experience
and experiment

THE UK BRANCH OF THE CALOUSTE GULBENKIAN FOUNDATION 1956–2006

experience
and experiment

THE UK BRANCH OF THE
CALOUSTE GULBENKIAN FOUNDATION 1956–2006

ROBERT HEWISON AND JOHN HOLDEN

CALOUSTE GULBENKIAN FOUNDATION
50 years 1956 2006

Published by the
Calouste Gulbenkian Foundation
United Kingdom Branch
98 Portland Place
London W1B 1ET
Tel: 020 7908 7604
Email: info@gulbenkian.org.uk
Website: www.gulbenkian.org.uk

The right of Robert Hewison and John Holden to be identified as the authors of this work has been
asserted in accordance with the Copyright, Designs and Patents Act 1988.

The publishers have made every effort to secure permission to reproduce material protected by
copyright. They will be pleased to make good any omissions brought to their attention in future printings
of this book.

ISBN 1 903080 05 3
ISBN (13) 9781 903080 05 4

British Library Cataloguing-in-Publication Data
A catalogue record for this book is available from the British Library.

Copyedited by James Loader
Designed by Helen Swansbourne
Printed by Expression Printers Ltd, IP23 8HH

Distributed by Central Books, 99 Wallis Road, London E9 5LN
Tel: 0845 458 9911, Fax: 0845 458 9912, Email: orders@centralbooks.com
Website: www.centralbooks.com

Cover image: Street party, Mozart Street, Liverpool 8, 1975. From *Survival Programmes: In Britain's Inner
Cities*, a major photographic study supported by the Foundation, published in 1982. Photo: © Paul Trevor,
Exit Photography Group project.

Frontispiece: Paula Rego, *Margaret and David*, 2003. Pastel on paper mounted on aluminium, 150 x 90 cm.
A painting of Queen Margaret, later St Margaret, and her son David (who became King David I of
Scotland), commissioned by Durham Cathedral, with support from the Foundation, for an altar dedicated
to the saint. Courtesy of the artist. Photo: Courtesy of the Chapter of Durham Cathedral.

Contents

Preface

This astutely written book is an absorbing read. It is not simply a tribute to over fifty years' extraordinary work of a small independent foundation, albeit the branch of a very large Lisbon-based organisation; it also reminds us how radically changed our lives have been over the past half-century. I find it particularly interesting to note how the Gulbenkian Foundation has reflected the sea-changes in the life of the nation, its own ethos evolving from straightforward enlightened paternalism right through to an enthusiasm for the radical that emerged with the spirit of the Sixties.

The early years of Thatcherism and serious political unrest found charities and foundations fire-fighting to develop new responses to deepening social rifts. Out of those years there emerged a spirit of greater self-reliance, maintained today in the Foundation's support of projects which encourage organisations and individuals to take more control of their own lives.

Just a glance at the text and photographs shows how grim things often were in the post-war years, and while, of course, poverty is still with us, as are injustice, rural deprivation and urban squalor, there have always been anarchic individuals with a vision of change. The Foundation has often recognised those with bold ideas, who founded organisations that went on to make an extraordinary impact on private and public life. Gulbenkian was an early supporter of Shelter, the Samaritans, the Runnymede Trust, and of such arts foundations as the Royal Shakespeare Company and Benjamin Britten's Snape Maltings, as well as, more recently, demonstrating the importance of the arts in the education of disaffected children. It has also always recognised the need to provide funding in the regions, helping, for example, to establish the first regional arts offices and a network of regional studio theatres where experiment could take place.

This history reminds us how small organisations can often be agile in taking risks and have a significant influence on larger organisations and on future government policy. Gulbenkian's research into children and violence was ahead of its time, as was its recognition of the strengths of a multicultural society, its advocacy of the importance of the arts in education, and of artists working with and learning from scientists, and I am sure it will continue to pioneer unexpected ideas.

Having been involved in the social, educational and cultural life of the country in different roles, I have come to know many who have benefited from Gulbenkian activity. Despite the fact that the Foundation is not a registered British charity, its work reflects British needs. In telling Gulbenkian's fifty-year history this story demonstrates its nature as part of the fabric of the UK.

Baroness Helena Kennedy QC

Introduction and acknowledgements

This brief history of the United Kingdom Branch of the Calouste Gulbenkian Foundation tells the story of a significantly successful venture. Since 1956, the Foundation has made interventions in the arts and culture, in social welfare and in education that have had profound and long-lasting effects. The list of organisations that the Gulbenkian has nurtured from its earliest days is both extensive and impressive. Politicians have been prodded into action; seminal publications have injected intellectual rigour and fresh thinking into the national debate; and the Foundation has created a forum for important discussions that have helped to shape the future of the public realm.

It will quickly become apparent that this is the story of a very unusual organisation. The Calouste Gulbenkian Foundation is one of the three or four largest foundations in Europe, but our account is limited to the activities of its United Kingdom Branch, which has undertaken a varying number of responsibilities on behalf of the main Foundation, a Portuguese charitable institution based in Lisbon. Although the United Kingdom Branch behaves in all respects like a British charity, it is not one, which helps to account for the independence of spirit it has shown. An account of the unique position from which the United Kingdom Branch has operated offers an opportunity to reflect on the way in which the role of the 'third sector' in British life – charities, foundations and voluntary bodies, as opposed to commerce or the state – has changed in the past fifty years.

The Foundation has always acted as a catalyst, a provoker of ideas, and it uses often quite small grants to launch schemes that, once proven, become part of mainstream thinking and are then taken up by organisations with deeper pockets and longer-term responsibilities for financial support. The Foundation has a well-established pattern of funding projects for a limited period, often publishing reports into the potential for new ways of working and entering into discussions with other agencies, both statutory and

OPPOSITE: Jazz singer Maria João at *Atlantic Waves 2001* (see page 209).
Photo: Miguel Faleiro.

9

voluntary, to develop further new streams of support and promotion. When it was established in 1956 the United Kingdom Branch was able to do much to support official policy in building up a post-war structure of support for the arts and social welfare; during the cultural, economic and political upheavals of the 1970s it was able to sustain the artistic and social gains made in the 1960s, while moving into a more critical relationship to government. In the 1980s the United Kingdom Branch, along with other British foundations and charities, was faced with the social and cultural problems created by a government determined to shrink the responsibilities

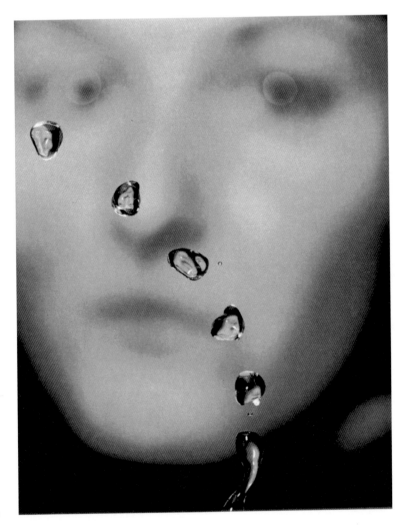

Arts: The cover image from the Foundation's publication *Strange and Charmed: Science and the contemporary visual arts*, 2000. Susan Derges, *The Observer and the Observed* (no. 6), 1991. Gelatin – silver print 71 x 61 cm. © Susan Derges. Photo: Courtesy of the artist and Purdy Hicks Gallery, London.

Arts: *Mapping the Edge*, site-specific theatre performance, Sheffield, 2001, created by wilson+wilson. Photo: Dominic Ibbotson.

of the state. Now, in the twenty-first century, it faces the challenge of a government that has once more taken up the social, educational and cultural issues of the day, thus narrowing the space for private initiative, while at the same time regulating public services, including those provided by the voluntary sector, through a regime of targets, tables and testing.

Even though this history is confined to just one area of the overall operations of the Gulbenkian Foundation, we have not been able to mention every social project, every art commission, every educational initiative that has involved the Gulbenkian in the United Kingdom, Ireland, and the Commonwealth. Past and present members of staff at Portland Place would also be the first to acknowledge that a great many of the activities that have been generated or supported have not been the exclusive property of the Branch, but have been achieved in partnership with other organisations. Some ideas have been initiated by the staff, some have been undertaken in response to outside appeals, and in many cases it is very difficult to say which element has been the most important in the outcome of the final project. Our criterion is simply that the United Kingdom Branch has been actively involved with all the projects, investigations, initiatives, seminars, conferences and publications that we describe, and this involvement has always gone much further than simply handing out money.

We have set out to evoke the 'personality' of the United Kingdom Branch, by tracing the drives and enthusiasms of its staff. We also believe that the decisions of an organism as intimate as a private foundation, but as publicly influential as the Gulbenkian, are best understood by setting them in the social and cultural context in which they were made. It has given us an opportunity to look at the history of Britain through three perspectives that are rarely brought together in the same frame. The Foundation is active in the field of the arts, education, and social welfare; together these account for a great deal of what can improve or decrease the quality of life. All three are subject, either positively or negatively, to the vicissitudes of public policy and public funding. That is why, in the chapters that follow, we have decided as far as possible to link rather than separate our accounts of the activities of the Branch's individual Departments. The frame that holds these narratives together is the history of an organisation without which Britain would be different, and lesser.

Since the United Kingdom Branch is very much an active organisation, we begin in the present, with a description of a meeting where decisions are taken and policy discussed. We explain how the Branch currently operates, and how it came to be established in the unique way that it was. Any private foundation will bear traces of the personality of its founder, so there is an account of the formation of the Calouste Gulbenkian Foundation in 1956 and the remarkable career of Calouste Sarkis Gulbenkian himself. The objectives of the Foundation were defined in the Founder's will, but it was up to the first members of the Board, notably Gulbenkian's English legal representative, Sir Charles Whishaw, who became the Trustee responsible for the United Kingdom Branch, to devise the structures that would make them achievable in the United Kingdom.

The second chapter, which covers the period 1956 to 1972, is defined by the successive directorships of Allen Sanderson and James Thornton, and the brief directorship of Alexander Dunbar before he took over the running of the Scottish Arts Council. In the 1950s Britain was in a mood of post-war

Education: M6 Theatre
Company perform
Forever by Mary
Cooper, a play about
parenting, 2001.
Photo: Ian Tilton.

reconstruction and the Branch was still finding its way. While establishing the Gulbenkian name through a number of landmark building projects, it was decided to concentrate on three strands of activity: the arts, which took up at least 50 per cent of its grants in the following years, and education and charity, which shared the remainder. It is significant that by 1969 the somewhat patronising term 'charity' had been replaced by the more pro-active 'social welfare'.

The Branch had found its direction in 1959 with the publication of its own specially commissioned report *Help for the Arts*, remembered as the Bridges Report, after the chairman of its investigating committee, Lord Bridges. This had been set up to advise the Foundation on the needs of the arts in post-war Britain, and to suggest ways in which the Gulbenkian could exercise its considerable patronage in an area where it was much needed. *Help for the Arts* not only proved to be the first of a series of highly influential reports on cultural policy that the United Kingdom Branch has

Education: Jenny Mosley, Director of the Quality Circle Time Model for All-Round
Success in Schools, conducts Quality Circle Time in a primary school, 2000.
Photo: Jenny Mosley Consultancies.

commissioned or co-funded, but also set a pattern by which it would bring together a team of experts to investigate an issue, draw up a policy and publish a report that would have an influence far beyond the immediate purposes of the Foundation.

The Gulbenkian's practice has always followed a consistent pattern: to engage, network, enquire, deliberate and then act; and it is one that has been repeated time and time again. In 1968 the Younghusband Report for the Foundation, *Community Work and Social Change*, had a profound effect in legitimating the emerging profession and practice of community work in Britain, and helped to crystallise the Foundation's long-term commitment to helping communities, especially the most vulnerable, to help themselves. During this period the Foundation gave important help to fledgling organisations that have since become major players: the Community Development Foundation, the Samaritans, and Shelter.

In the 1960s the Bridges Report had a significant impact on the cultural infrastructure of Britain. Not only had the report suggested innovations such as artists' residences (commonplace now, but then a radical idea), it had adopted a nationwide, non-metropolitan outlook that led in particular to the formation of the Regional Arts Associations. This established the long tradition of the Gulbenkian giving help to projects well away from the main centres of influence. Between 1956 and the mid-1970s the Foundation spent the equivalent of more than £20 million at today's values on building theatres, arts centres and galleries across the United Kingdom. At this period, with responsibility for helping organisations in the British Commonwealth, the United Kingdom Branch was also contributing to similar arts-building and cultural and educational projects overseas. In a landmark collaboration with the Tate Gallery the Foundation sponsored the first international survey of post-war art in 1964, and substantially paid for the construction of new galleries at the Tate that were to open in 1979.

Our third chapter begins in January 1972, with the arrival of a new Director, Peter Brinson, and closes with his departure in 1982. The period was one of anxiety and depression in Britain following the optimistic, expansionist mood of the 1960s, and ended with the arrival of a Conservative government that was determined to change the relationship between the individual, the community, and the state. Brinson's distinctive personality, as well as the nature of the period of his directorship, justifies his being given a single chapter. An aesthete, with a profound passion for dance, Brinson was also a radical, determined to act in the defence of values that came increasingly under pressure after the election of Mrs Thatcher in 1979. His watchword was 'community', and he made sure that the United Kingdom Branch's three Departments worked closely together on that theme. The Foundation could no longer afford to support the cost of new buildings, and instead put its energies into giving practical support to increasingly beleaguered groups by encouraging community arts, community enterprise, and self-education. In one area, in spite of the substantial efforts made, the Foundation did not succeed, when it proved unable to overcome vested interests in order to set up a national centre for community work. At the same time, however, the United Kingdom Branch, concerned by the rising racial tension in Britain in the early 1970s, sought to provide the means for West Indian and Asian interest groups to come together for the first time to fight racism. The National Organisation of African, Asian and Caribbean People proved short-lived, but significant work was done in helping the independent Runnymede Trust, the Joint Council for the Welfare of Immigrants, and the government's Community Relations Commission.

In 1976 the United Kingdom Branch sponsored two important reports. One, by Naseem Khan, *The Arts Britain Ignores*, addressed the cultural issues linked to the racial tensions Britain was experiencing. The other, *Support for the Arts in England and Wales*, published by the Foundation and known by the name of its chairman as the Redcliffe-Maud Report, showed how far Britain's cultural infrastructure had developed since the Bridges Report of 1959 – and how much further there was to go. The United Kingdom Branch was no longer in a position to act on its own, and right across the board, from the arts, to education to social welfare, it found itself working with others to achieve common goals. In spite of its more limited financial reach, however, it did have a substantial impact in the field of dance, virtually creating the contemporary dance scene in Britain, funding commissions for choreographers and composers, as well as experiments with new technologies. Throughout its existence the Foundation has had a commitment to encouraging contemporary artists of all kinds, from Benjamin Britten in the 1950s, to the young Portuguese artists featured in this century's annual *Atlantic Waves* festival. It also has a strong tradition of encouraging the vocational training of artists of all disciplines.

It was during Brinson's directorship that the United Kingdom Branch's offices in Portland Place became famous for their hospitality. This was a means of influencing politicians, and forming alliances with other agencies. It was also during Brinson's time that the *Annual Report* became an important vehicle for communicating the Foundation's ideas and principles. The Foundation has always been transparent in the approach it has taken to applications for funds, and the care it has shown for successful and unsuccessful applicants alike. Some of its full and influential reports have already been mentioned, to which should be added Lord Boyle's *Current Issues in Community Work* of 1973 and Lady Seear's *Community Business Works* of 1982. In 1977 the appointment of a Literary Editor led to a substantial expansion in the United Kingdom Branch's publications programme. A full list of its publications is given on pages 218–220, and from that it is possible to see that the Foundation has not only put ideas into practice, but also put practice into print, thus ensuring that the lessons learned from the hundreds of short-term and experimental projects with which the Gulbenkian has been involved are not lost. Unhampered by the need to turn a profit, the Gulbenkian has become a niche publisher in its own right – as this book shows.

The final report that Brinson was associated with as Director was in the field of education: Ken Robinson's *The Arts in Schools* of 1982. The Foundation had long fought to support the presence of art and artists in schools, and this report served to moderate the technological ambitions of those planning the new National Curriculum. It became a key document for those resisting the exclusion of imagination and creativity from education, as we show. Here, as occasionally elsewhere in the book, we have found it helpful to trace the development and later history of a project in order to complete the account.

Chapter four begins in October 1982, at a time of significant internal and external change for the Gulbenkian Foundation. The Foundation in Lisbon had weathered the storm of the Portuguese revolution of 1974, and by 1981 it was felt that some reallocation of responsibilities was necessary. The United Kingdom Branch continued its work in the United Kingdom and the Republic of Ireland, but responsibility for activities in the Commonwealth was transferred to Lisbon. At the same time a new Anglo-Portuguese Cultural Relations Programme was launched. The United Kingdom Branch has always looked after the interests of Gulbenkian staff and visitors in Britain, those studying on Gulbenkian visiting scholarships, and those in the UK for medical treatment, but it was felt that more should be done for the Portuguese community in Britain, and for the promotion of Portuguese culture. An account of how this Programme has developed up till now is given in our final chapter. There were also important changes of personnel. Sir Charles Whishaw retired as the Gulbenkian's London Trustee in 1981, and was replaced by Mikhael Essayan, QC, grandson of the Founder. In 1982 L.C. ('Kim') Taylor became the new Director.

As a former teacher, Taylor had a particular interest in education, and the United Kingdom Branch was much involved in the debates leading up to the Education Reform Act of 1988, shifting its attention from older students to early childhood and the under-18s. There was considerable synergy between

Social Welfare: 'Nothing decided about us, without us.' Help the Aged's 'Speaking Up For Our Age' national conference in 2004, where delegates addressed problems facing older people, such as transport issues, pensions, council tax and health care.
Photo: Help the Aged.

Social Welfare:
Cawley Maintenance
was assisted in 2004
by Street(UK), which
helps entrepreneurs set
up small businesses.
Photo: Street(UK).

the activities of the Education Department and the Arts Department, where the long-standing commitment to training led to investment in the development of the neglected skills of circus and puppetry. The Foundation also made a substantial contribution to the development of Public Art – a response to the perceived decay in the public realm – and to the new field linking the benefits of access to the arts in public health. The Social Welfare Department meanwhile worked hard to ameliorate the effects of local government reorganisation on the voluntary sector, and the substantial growth in poverty, unemployment and deprivation during the 1980s. The need for regeneration following the industrial restructuring of the decade was implicit in the title of John Myerscough's *The Economic Importance of the Arts in Britain*, a highly influential report initiated by the United Kingdom Branch, and published in 1988.

Taylor retired as Director in 1988, but because there is so much continuity in the work being undertaken at this time, we have combined the period of his directorship with that of his successor, the former MP, Ben Whitaker, ending chapter four with Whitaker's retirement in 1999. Taylor and Whitaker both took a particular interest in the United Kingdom Branch's activities in Ireland, both sides of the border, where few other foundations were active during the most troubled times for the island. Whitaker also had an enthusiasm for museums. Children, who suffered especially from the deprivations engendered in the 1980s, continued to be a priority, and in 1991 the Branch published a report, *Taking Children Seriously: A proposal for a Children's Rights Commissioner*, which began a long struggle for the recognition of children's rights at senior government level that was only concluded in 2005. Violence against children, whether bullying by other children or any of the degrees of harm inflicted by adults, from smacking upwards, became a major concern for the Foundation and its reports and enquiries had a significant effect on policy and public opinion. When it drew attention to the plight of children obliged to act as carers for their disabled parents the Foundation showed that it was once again able to recognise a social need that the public authorities had largely overlooked.

In education, a Foundation report, *Moving Culture* (1990), helped to increase public understanding of the creativity contained in what was ordinarily dismissed as consumerist youth culture, and true to the Branch's tradition, a successful campaign was mounted to restore a nationwide right to public funding for dance and drama students. In the 1990s the United Kingdom Branch, having been much concerned with the inner cities in the 1980s, turned its attention to the unrecognised social deprivation that existed in the countryside. The Arts Department managed an exemplary and innovative scheme to stimulate small-scale, largely non-professional rural arts activities. In 1995 it began to develop a new strand of work, encouraging artists to engage with the new technical and cultural possibilities offered by science. Having brought out the material value of investment in the arts with the 1988 report, *The Economic Importance of the Arts in Britain*, in 1997 it redressed the balance by helping to fund the think-tank Comedia's examination of the social, as opposed to the economic, benefits that flow from cultural activity, in the report *Use or Ornament? The social impact of participation in the arts*.

Our final chapter brings the history of the United Kingdom Branch up to the present day. In 1999 Paula Ridley took over as Director, and introduced considerable internal changes, cutting down administrative costs and refocusing the Anglo-Portuguese Cultural Relations Programme, whose great success in finding an audience for contemporary Portuguese culture in Britain we describe here. The Branch has made a major public statement with the establishment of the largest arts prize in Britain, the £100,000 Gulbenkian Prize for Museums and Galleries. The Prize shows continuity as well as innovation, however, for museums have been a long-standing interest of the Foundation, which reflects the Founder's interests. Similarly the Arts Department continues to support experiment and exploration by individual artists, while the Education Department is working to help the most deprived in the education system – those pupils who have been permanently or temporarily excluded from their schools – and the Social Welfare Department continues to be concerned with social policy and to help communities to help themselves.

Having sought to demonstrate, throughout the book, how the United Kingdom Branch works, both technically as an organisation that has had to adapt to the shifting currents of public policy, and intellectually as one that has consistently supported experiment in the arts, self-empowerment in the community, and innovation in education, we conclude by trying to show *why* the Gulbenkian works, how it has successfully developed procedures of investigation and publication and how it has always been as interested in the people who can make a project work as in the social or educational theory behind it. It may well be that, as the financial power of the United Kingdom Branch has shrunk, its influence has grown, as it has had to work ever more collaboratively with other organisations. Its successes have far outweighed its failures, and where there have been failures, that is only because the Foundation has used its independence, its imagination, and its philanthropic commitment, to take risks.

Our narrative is based on archive material, on the remarkably full and historically informative *Annual Report* (a good example of a private foundation's public transparency), on the Foundation's own publications (a vital part of its operations), and on interviews with past and present members of the United Kingdom Branch's staff. We would like to thank Sir Charles Whishaw for permission to reprint extracts from his private memoir, which concerns both his work for the Founder, Calouste Sarkis Gulbenkian, and his long service as the Foundation's first London Trustee. We also thank Dr Helen Crummy, Robin Guthrie, Lord Feversham, Elisabeth Littlejohn, Peter Stark and Professor George Wedell who gave us permission to quote

Anglo-Portuguese Cultural Relations: Eça de Queirós, whose volume of *English Letters*, written while he was Portuguese Consul in London between 1874 and 1888, was published by Carcanet in 2000. Photo: Editorial Caminho, Lisbon.

passages from their correspondence with Richard Mills. We are most grateful to Mikhael Essayan and Martin Essayan, past and present London Trustees, for the courtesy and openness with which they have treated us. We would like to thank Millicent Bowerman, Paul Curno, Fiona Ellis, Iain Reid, Kim Taylor and Ben Whitaker for their recollections of their times at Portland Place. The present staff, led by the Director, Paula Ridley, has been both hospitable and helpful, in the Gulbenkian tradition. Paula Ridley and her departmental Directors Siân Ede, Simon Richey and Miguel Santos have answered all our questions and allowed us to witness the inner workings of the Branch. The Head of Publications, Felicity Luard, and the Information Officer, Louisa Hooper, have not only seen the book through the press, but given us every possible help along the way. We would also like to thank

Anglo-Portuguese
Cultural Relations:
Percussion ensemble
Bombos de Santo
André performing
during the Glen Lyon
Millennium Project in
Scotland, *The Path*,
2000, staged by nva.
Photo: © Alan
McAteer.

Jayne Anne Eustace O'Flynn, Jascha Elliott and Barry Chorlton for making
sure that every visit to Portland Place has been an enjoyable one.

There have been two earlier accounts of the activities of the Gulbenkian
Foundation's United Kingdom Branch, the contributions of both of which we
would like to acknowledge. *Twenty-One Years* was published by the Foundation in 1977, and gave a summary of the Branch's activities since 1956. In
1996 the Directory of Social Change published David N. Thomas's *Oil on
Troubled Waters: The Gulbenkian Foundation and social welfare*. As the title
suggests, this thorough study concentrated on the Branch's Social Welfare
Programme: it is an invaluable guide to the development of social policy in
Britain, and contains detailed information about, and analysis of, the distribution of social welfare grants. This new history, however, is the first attempt
to give a comprehensive overview of a unique institution, and we are very
grateful for the opportunity it has afforded us to explore a relatively little-
known, but vital, aspect of public life. We acknowledge our errors of omission,
and hope that any errors of commission will be forgiven.

Robert Hewison, John Holden

CHAPTER 1

How the Gulbenkian works

'A Foundation, unless it has narrowly confined objects, will always reflect the thoughts and preferences and, if it is not too pompous a word, the vision of those charged with the task of running it. No two people, no two groups of people would reach the same decisions. What a dull world it would be if it were so.'

SIR CHARLES WHISHAW, TRUSTEE

PREFACE TO *TWENTY-ONE YEARS*, 1977

OPPOSITE: **The Foundation's UK Branch offices at 98 Portland Place, London.**

London, 15 March 2005

We ring the doorbell at 98 Portland Place and are welcomed into the grand but discreet premises of the Calouste Gulbenkian Foundation's United Kingdom Branch. A Trustee meeting is to be held this morning, and the small staff gathers in the Committee Room. Coffee and biscuits travel round the table; papers are ordered and shuffled. At the head sits Mikhael Essayan QC, grandson of the Founder, for what will be his penultimate meeting as the Foundation's single Trustee based in London – his son, Martin Essayan, a 45-year-old business strategist, will take over the role in August.

This is the 268th in a series of meetings stretching back to 1956: meetings to determine who will receive grants from the Foundation. Although everyone in the room – except one – is British, the Foundation is in fact Portuguese, with its substantial headquarters, including a museum, a modern art centre, auditoria and conference facilities, in an eighteen-acre park in Lisbon. That is why there is only one UK Trustee, who will take his decisions and recommendations to the main Board. Under Portuguese law the Trustees are known as 'Executive Administrators', with each having a

Mikhael Essayan, UK Trustee, 1981–2005 (left), and Martin Essayan, UK Trustee from 2005 (right). Photos: Hazel Thompson – True Image.

specific area of executive responsibility in a more commercial model of governance that gives them an administrative control not afforded to the volunteer trustees of British charities.

There is a great store of knowledge and expertise in the room. A gold pen ticks approvals, as Essayan's lawyer's eyes spot spelling gaffes and he questions jargon: what is 'scenario planning'? How will 'key drivers of change' translate into Portuguese? The pace is brisk, but genial. There are jokes: will an opera project explore new areas, or new arias? But the meeting is purposeful and earnest. From social deprivation to groundbreaking art, the subjects dealt with are serious ones, for the Foundation has a reputation to maintain, and a history to live up to.

'Mr Five Per Cent'

Calouste Sarkis Gulbenkian was an Armenian born in Turkey in 1869, his father a trader and banker in Scutari. A graduate in engineering at King's College London, in 1902 Gulbenkian became, and thereafter remained, a British citizen, conducting much of his work from London and then Paris, but finally settling in Portugal. The source of his immense wealth was oil: he spotted the potential for oil exploration in Mesopotamia, then part of the Ottoman Empire, now Iraq. Wheeling and dealing with French, American and Anglo-Dutch companies, he secured a 5 per cent share of the revenues of what became in 1929 the Iraq Petroleum Company – hence his friendly nickname. In 1927 he settled in Paris, where his house at 51 avenue d'Iéna (still owned by the Foundation) became famous for his collection of books, coins, manuscripts, paintings, statues and other *objets d'art*. He also became a private benefactor to the Armenian community across the world.

Gulbenkian lent paintings to the National Gallery in London, and became a close friend of its pre-war Director, Kenneth Clark. In 1937 he offered to leave his entire collection, supported by his oil wealth, to create a Gulbenkian Annexe to the National Gallery, but the outbreak of war in 1939 interrupted negotiations. While his masterpieces went into store in Wales with the rest of the National Gallery collection, Gulbenkian decided to stay in Paris. As a commercial adviser to the Persian (today, Iranian) government

Calouste Sarkis Gulbenkian at 24 and (opposite) 81 years.

he held a diplomatic passport, and after the fall of France in 1940 he travelled with their mission to Vichy. The vicissitudes of war (and the struggle to control oil interests in the Middle East) led this very pro-British man to be classed as an 'enemy alien', and his oil shares were vested in the Custodian of Enemy Property. In 1942 Gulbenkian was allowed to leave France for neutral Portugal, and in 1943 his shares were released, but although negotiations over his possible gift to the National Gallery continued, they came to nothing after Kenneth Clark's departure as Director in 1945, meaning the loss of an endowment that would have completely transformed the fortunes of the gallery. In 1950 Gulbenkian's paintings were transferred on loan to the National Gallery in Washington, where they remained until 1969 while a home was prepared for them in Lisbon.

OPPOSITE: Aerial view of the Calouste Gulbenkian Park, Lisbon, with the Foundation's Headquarters (right foreground), Museum (left foreground), and Modern Art Centre (centre).

Finding the climate and the tax regime congenial, and Lisbon, according to his London solicitor Charles Whishaw, 'a comfortable and quiet refuge away from prying press', Gulbenkian stayed in Portugal until his death in 1955. The bulk of his fortune, which included the continuing 5 per cent from Iraqi oil, generating about £4 million a year, was left to create the Foundation that commemorates his name. Unfortunately his son Nubar challenged the will, and Gulbenkian's first choice of Chairman, his close friend and legal adviser Lord Radcliffe, declined the role. Instead his politically astute Portuguese lawyer, Dr José de Azeredo Perdigão, took over, and ran the Foundation for the next thirty-five years. The Foundation was registered as a charity under United States tax law. Following a visit to Iraq, Perdigão wisely concluded that Middle Eastern oil revenues might not be the most stable of investments. Before Iraq completed the nationalisation of its oil in 1972, the Trustees used their income to buy a portfolio of mainly US dollar-based assets that would in turn provide the wherewithal to support the Foundation's objectives. The house in Paris remained as a cultural centre, there would be provision for the Armenian Diaspora, the people of Portugal would be beneficiaries as hosts to the Foundation, its collection and activities, and the interests of Britain and the British Commonwealth would be represented by a United Kingdom Branch.

2005

The 268th London Trustee meeting is drawing to a close. Led by the United Kingdom Branch's Director, Paula Ridley, those responsible for the four Departments – Arts, Social Welfare, Education and Anglo-Portuguese Cultural Relations – have presented their recommendations for £700,000 worth of grants, representing almost a third of the planned grant expenditure for the year. Although the atmosphere in the room is relaxed, these

meetings – held three or four times a year – represent a great deal of work for the Directors, and each will have spent some time preparing the papers for the meeting. Some applications can be rejected by the staff because they fall outside the Foundation's guidelines, as declared in its annual leaflet *Advice to Applicants for Grants for the UK and Ireland*. But those that do qualify have to be investigated through letters and telephone calls, visits may be made to projects and there will be seminars and conferences to attend to keep abreast of the field. Personal contact is vital: there will be conversations not only with the applicants, but with the literally hundreds of experts and advisers that are called upon over the course of a year. Contact will continue once an application has succeeded. The United Kingdom Branch makes less use of formal advisory committees than it used to, since the best people are the busiest and the hardest to get together, but it still uses steering groups for particular projects.

For qualifying applications, confirmation of acceptance or rejection remains with Essayan as Trustee, but it is not his practice to initiate projects, so that policy is driven by the staff, who are professionals in their fields and responsive to developments and new needs within their areas of expertise. Essayan's decision will be based on a paper prepared by a staff member, and there will have been informal consideration before today's meeting. Essayan currently agrees grants of £15,000 or less on the spot; larger ones will go to Lisbon for the next meeting of the full Board, but disagreement with the Board is rare. Although it is dependent on an annual decision to continue its funding, the United Kingdom Branch enjoys considerable autonomy from Lisbon, and, while choosing to act as if it were a UK charity, it is not obliged to follow the procedures of British charity law.

In the Committee Room, questions are raised about the administration of one grant; the policy of another organisation is praised. As always, people round the table are aware that, unlike the Arts Council or a government department, they cannot take on projects for which there would have to be long-term revenue funding. Miguel Santos, responsible for Anglo-Portuguese Cultural Relations, warns of developing an 'ad aeternum situation' by continuing a particular grant. Information that the Arts Council now puts substantial resources into the arts and health means that the Foundation, once the pioneer in this field, can move its resources elsewhere. In a discussion of a potentially controversial award Siân Ede, Deputy Director and in charge of the arts portfolio, argues that there has to be an element of risk, while Ridley comments that 'these are responsible people'. Essayan concludes: 'I will draw the Board's attention to this . . .'

The Shaping of History

Looking back over the last fifty years, the broad political, social and economic environment in which the Foundation's United Kingdom Branch has operated has passed through four distinct phases. The period from 1956 to the early 1970s was essentially one of post-war growth, prosperity and optimism, accompanied by growing social liberalism. Deference declined, experimentation increased. But in the early 1970s all this began to unravel. In the economy, hyperinflation led to the three-day week, mass unemployment and strikes. Weak governments – four Prime Ministers, two Labour, two Conservative, in the space of ten years – were both a cause and effect of this economic and social malaise. A third phase began with the election of the Conservative government in 1979, when the post-war political consensus was abandoned. Assumptions about the respective roles of foundations, the voluntary sector and government were completely overturned, while the emphasis on market solutions and the primacy of the individual had profound effects. The latest phase began when New Labour came to power in 1997, with a rhetoric of renewed interest in ideas of mutuality, society and communal solutions. Despite low interest rates and low unemployment, and an economic landscape that offered stability, there remained no lack of social problems to be addressed.

The Foundation was inevitably affected by its context: inflation, unemployment, cuts in government expenditure and the rest changed both the demands that were placed upon it by grant applicants and its own ability to meet those applicants' needs. Consequently the Foundation's financial muscle in relation to government spending has consistently declined over the last half-century. The most obvious example is in relation to the Arts Council. In 1960 the Foundation's arts budget was 11.6 per cent of that of the Arts Council (£174,680 as opposed to £1,500,000). In 1970 the proportion had fallen to 3.8 per cent, whilst in 2004 it had dropped to 0.15

per cent (respectively £744,000 for the Foundation and £496,110,000 for the Arts Council, including £153 million from the National Lottery).

That said, so much of the Arts Council's budget has been tied into the long-term funding of its clients that the discretional spending of the Arts Council and of the Foundation bear comparison. This freedom from the obligations of institutional maintenance has enabled the Foundation to use its resources to change the policy context of governments. It has always been, and continues to be, a leader. The private nature of charitable and educational foundations means that they can act where government holds back. As former United Kingdom Branch Director Ben Whitaker commented in his study *The Foundations*, they are able to 'finance ideas that are politically valuable but which are thought to be as yet too politically sensitive'. This has been fully recognised, and indeed embraced with relish, by the Gulbenkian. As the 1982 *Annual Report* states: 'Foundations have their own job to do in exploring new ideas, taking initiatives and taking risks which the spenders of taxpayers' and ratepayers' money perhaps cannot take.'

The Gulbenkian's United Kingdom Branch has fulfilled this role of being an innovator by backing pathfinder projects, seeking out the innovative and unusual, and influencing government policy and professional practice. In other words it has embraced both ends of a problem, providing funding to give practical help to the most disadvantaged in society while corralling the Great and the Good to apply influence and intelligence to change attitudes and, sometimes, legislation. This has led to a curious conjunction, as a distinguished contributor to more than one Gulbenkian committee of enquiry has recorded:

> What I particularly recall of my connections with the Foundation is the combination of extreme formality, propriety and palatial surroundings with the astonishing inventiveness and creativity of the staff and Trustee. More than perhaps any other foundation the Gulbenkian has reached out to people in the situations in which they are struggling to operate and survive ... At all points the Foundation managed to link the highest to the lowest, whether it was high art to community art, or high policy to street problems. People sometimes failed to understand the nature of this achievement, and the extraordinary anomalies it sometimes gave rise to – I think, for example, of the splendid dinner at the Savoy to mark the work of the group led by Lord Boyle [*Current Issues in Community Work*, 1973]. That whole exercise was unique and typically Gulbenkian.

The recollection is by Robin Guthrie, Director of the Joseph Rowntree Memorial Trust between 1979 and 1988, and Chief Charity Commissioner for England and Wales between 1988 and 1992, writing to the United Kingdom Branch's former Deputy Director, Richard Mills, in 1992.

In parallel with the wider historical context runs the story of the personalities and enthusiasms of particular Directors of the Foundation's United Kingdom Branch. As Mikhael Essayan told us, 'The London Trustee always keeps a low profile. If you have a skilled professional staff they are the people who ought to be looking for things to do.' As has been noted, the London Trustee and the Branch's staff have considerable autonomy, and each Director has left his or her mark, whether it be James Thornton's interest in archaeology, Peter Brinson's passion for dance or Ben Whitaker's love for Ireland. Deputy and Assistant Directors have been allowed to follow their personal enthusiasms. It is one of the things that has made the Foundation such a creative place throughout its first fifty years.

1956: First Steps

In its earliest days the United Kingdom Branch had to find its feet. Following the withdrawal of Lord Radcliffe, the Foundation's first Trustees, in addition to Perdigão, were Gulbenkian's son-in-law Kevork Essayan; the anglophile Duke of Palmella; Dr Theotónio Pereira, Portuguese Ambassador to London; and Charles (later, Sir Charles) Whishaw, who had been Gulbenkian's man of business in London and had been particularly effective when his oil assets were sequestrated during the war. The Foundation's statutes allow for there always to be one member of the Gulbenkian family on the Board.

Assisted by Pereira until his return to Lisbon to join the Salazar government, Whishaw became the London Trustee. As a partner in the firm of Freshfields and a member of the Council of the Law Society, he found in the Foundation an outlet for the more liberal sympathies that his public responsibilities tended to muffle. He has deposited with the United Kingdom Branch's archive the typescript of an amusing and illuminating memoir, 'A Kind of Lawyer', in which he describes the creation of the Foundation and his earlier days with the man he affectionately called 'Mr CSG'.

Mikhael Essayan (left)
and Sir Charles
Whishaw (right) with
Millicent Bowerman
at a Foundation lunch
in 1981.

Whishaw records that he suspected Gulbenkian 'had no very clear idea of what he really wanted for his Foundation, and he certainly had no idea of the surge in oil production which would transform what would, at the time of the will, have been a modestly endowed foundation with a fine personal art collection, into a major international foundation'. Whishaw's difficulties were compounded by the fact that neither Pereira nor he 'had any experience in running a charity, nor indeed the time to do so'. Accordingly they sought the advice of the Director of the Nuffield Foundation, Dr Leslie Farrar Brown, who recommended that they appoint as Foundation Secretary one of Brown's own staff, Allen Sanderson. Slight, almost frail, but a phenomenal worker with a very quick and retentive brain, Oxford-educated Sanderson had served in wartime intelligence before becoming a Deputy Director at the Nuffield. Sanderson brought with him his personal assistant, Betty Hyams, who ten years later took on responsibility for Education, Science and Archaeology. According to Whishaw, Sanderson 'was just the right person to get us started; he knew all about procedures and had an imaginative approach to his task. It would not be easy; the will was not really helpful and the statutes of the Foundation simply followed the terms of the will'.

These stated that the Foundation was to pursue objectives relating to 'the Arts; Social Welfare and General Charity; Education and Science', but that did not get them very far, and the Board in Lisbon laid down no guidelines, 'recognising that the needs of each country, each activity, would surely differ. Applications, once they started, came in faster than we might have expected and we had inevitably to look at them all after Allen [Sanderson] had tabulated them', Whishaw recorded. While it was clear that there was plenty of scope in the arts, education and charity, the recent war and the needs of a modern industrial economy meant that science was relatively well funded by the government and other foundations. As Whishaw wrote: 'It did not take long for us to realise that in the world of science in the widest terms there would be virtually nothing we could usefully do.' Accordingly, apart from supporting a few scientific expeditions and other projects in the early years, science was put to one side until the 1990s, when the needs of what was now called the creative, as opposed to the industrial, economy called for an exploration of the linkages between science and art.

'General charity' was too vague a category; as an *Annual Report* noted in 1971: 'Unlike central or local government, a private foundation cannot accept responsibility towards the whole range of human endeavour,' and, as we will show, the somewhat patronising notion of 'charity' was replaced by 'social welfare'. Over the years, the Arts, Social Welfare and Education became a mutually supportive triumvirate. Reading through the details of grants given during the last fifty years, it is often difficult to categorise them rigidly between the three Programmes. In practice, many Arts projects will have a social welfare or community flavour and an educational focus. In 2004, for example, a grant of £25,000 was made to Doncaster Community Arts to write and publish an advice booklet for teachers in Pupil Referral Units (centres where young people who have been excluded from school are educated) on how to plan and implement residences by artists. This came out of the Education budget, but could have been classified equally well as either an Arts or Social Welfare project. The management structure of the United Kingdom Branch is like the spokes of a wheel, with the Director –

often also responsible for one sector, as Paula Ridley is for Social Welfare at present – at the hub, and the work of the Assistant Directors forming the rim.

From the earliest days there has been a consistent concern that applicants be treated with care and courtesy. Whishaw recalled that Sanderson 'had an unusual knack of going in alongside the applicant, and for recognising quality in some very inarticulate and badly presented applications'. The Foundation does not use complicated forms, relying on a simple letter and the judgement of the staff, although applicants have to be able to show they are registered charities or similar organisations. The inevitable fact is that most foundations receive more, sometimes vastly more, applications for funding than they can possibly accept. In the face of a torrent of supplication, some trusts are overwhelmed, and some become arrogant, but the Gulbenkian's approach and aspiration have been, as stated in the 1980 *Annual Report*, 'to guarantee a sympathetic reception to seekers after help and a caring response even to those who cannot be helped'. As a former Assistant Director, Arts, Fiona Ellis, told us, there is a 'Gulbenkian heritage of saying no nicely. Because care was taken to explain our reasons, I found that refusals were accepted in a way they sometimes aren't in the public sector.'

The United Kingdom Branch has learned to be transparent about its own affairs, so that since they began to be published in 1971, the Gulbenkian's *Annual Reports* have become a guide to the Foundation's thinking and future plans, as well as a record of grants awarded. As it declared in 1971: 'A private foundation enjoys a privileged position in public affairs. It is therefore right that it should explain to those particularly concerned and to the public generally what it is doing and how it has spent its money.'

Above all, the very security of being an independent, private foundation has meant that it has always been ready to take a risk: 'Being responsible to no-one save its Founder's intentions, a foundation acquires obligations consequent upon this "irresponsibility". It becomes by nature a body fitted to take risks, innovate, foster new ideas, act as a ginger force on other bodies whose "responsibility" prevents them sometimes seeing enough of the new for the old.' That was written in 1973, and the Foundation has built its reputation on always seeking out new areas of work or concern, investigating them thoroughly, and taking action, in the hope that slower-moving government agencies will follow, or that a long-term solution not dependent on its funding can be found. As Paula Ridley told us, 'The Gulbenkian was always up for something new – and I'd like to keep it that way.'

It was a risk to invite two independent writers to investigate the history of the Gulbenkian Foundation's United Kingdom Branch. This is what we found.

CHAPTER 2

Building bridges

1956–1972

'Unlike public bodies, trusts are accountable to themselves only. They give decisions but do not have to give reasons. This gives them a freedom of which they should make the fullest use.'

THE BRIDGES REPORT, HELP FOR THE ARTS, 1959

The first task for the staff of the United Kingdom Branch was to define its areas of activity: the Arts, Social Welfare and Education. As described in this chapter, over the first fifteen years the Foundation helped to build both the physical and institutional infrastructure of the arts: new theatres and galleries, the Regional Arts Associations, and support for artists, writers, musicians and composers. The invidious term 'charity' was replaced by 'social welfare', indicating a move away from the relief of need to the removal of its causes. The principal focus of the Education Programme was at university level. We will describe how the United Kingdom Branch developed an effective way of addressing problems by identifying an issue, conducting an enquiry, formulating a policy and carrying it through into action.

OPPOSITE: The concert hall at Snape Maltings to which the Foundation contributed £25,000 in 1966.
Photo: Clive Strutt.

For much of its first fifty years the Foundation has committed half of its annual income to cultural projects, and the role of the arts has been crucial in supporting other areas of activity. Of the four areas identified in the founding statutes – the Arts, Education, Charity and Science – the arts are most clearly identified with the private interests of 'Mr CSG', collector and connoisseur.

1956 was a good year in which to take up the cause of the arts. As Britain at last began to shed the drabness and deference of post-war austerity and caution, there were stirrings throughout the *avant-garde*, emblematised by the arrival of John Osborne's Angry Young Man in *Look Back in Anger* at the Royal Court Theatre. But, as a fledgling organisation, the Gulbenkian was not yet ready to take the bold risks it was to take in the later 1960s and 1970s. As Sir Charles Whishaw freely admitted in his memoir: 'Early grants were certainly non-controversial and unlikely to cause criticism.' But then official arts policy in Britain was hardly controversial either. National responsibility lay with the Arts Council of Great Britain, covering England, Scotland and Wales, though not Northern Ireland. Ten years after it had been founded, the ACGB's grant-in-aid for 1956/7 stood at £885,000. Calouste Gulbenkian's old friend Kenneth Clark was Chairman, and his patrician tastes did not conflict with the stated funding policy of its Secretary-General, W.E. Williams, in the Council's 1951 *Annual Report*: 'Few, but roses'.

The ACGB's roses included the Royal Opera House, Covent Garden, with its resident opera and ballet companies, which with Sadler's Wells Opera absorbed half the Council's annual grant. There was as yet no National Theatre or Royal Shakespeare Company, although their precursors were in existence at the Old Vic in London and the Shakespeare Memorial Theatre at Stratford. In 1956 the Council funded twenty-two regional repertory theatres, but over a hundred regional theatres had closed since the war, and more were to follow. In England four leading regional and two London symphony orchestras received funding of £100,000 between them, with about £30,000 going to other events and activities, including the regions. Visual art was supported through London and touring exhibitions, and there was a modest budget to buy works of art. Scotland got about £60,000 in all, Wales £23,000. The Council had withdrawn from the regional network of offices that it had inherited from its wartime predecessor, the Council for the Encouragement of Music and the Arts, and organisations outside London received only £221,000 in total, so the imbalance between London and the English regions was extreme.

While the British Council represented the arts abroad, the British Film Institute looked after cinema and the BBC played its own independent and significant role as cultural patron, the rest of the funding system consisted of the national museums and art galleries, directly funded by the government at about £3 million a year, and their regional counterparts, dependent on local authorities. As well as being responsible for the public library system, local authorities also maintained a variety of halls and theatres, from the good to the down-at-heel, but on average spent only a twentieth of the sixpenny (2.5 new pence) rate they were empowered to spend on the arts. Lord Bridges's 1959 report for the Gulbenkian concluded that local authorities were 'only marginal instead of major patrons of the arts'. Although the Festival of Britain in 1951 had brought the word 'contemporary' into fashionable use, in 1956 official cultural policy remained metropolitan in outlook, mandarin in taste.

While the state, sometimes grudgingly, and sometimes at the Foundation's prompting, has taken increasing responsibility for the arts in Britain, the Foundation has concentrated on finding new ways, not simply to fill the gaps, but to seed the experiments that lead to new work and new organisations. There are signs of what was to come even in the earliest half-dozen grants – £4,000 to Benjamin Britten's English Opera Group, which had seceded from Sadler's Wells; and £5,000 over three years for Ballet Rambert, then just about the only ballet company outside Covent Garden, an award that set a precedent for the Foundation's transformative support for contemporary dance in the 1970s. The Bluecoat Society of Arts in Liverpool got £2,000 a year for three years to fund a local artist and to organise a conference on the arts. A sign of the times was £6,425 to maintain seven refugee Hungarian music and art students taking courses in Britain, following the failed Hungarian uprising of 1956.

Three Arts grants went to buildings: after wartime and post-war neglect, Britain's theatres and galleries were run-down; but the Foundation also recognised that if it was to become better known, it would need, if only at first, to undertake projects to which its name could, actually, be attached. Accordingly, in April 1957 it announced a grant of £60,000 to the School of

One of the Foundation's first grants, in 1957, was £60,000 towards the cost of building the Gulbenkian Museum of Oriental Art at the University of Durham.
Photo: Reproduced by permission of Durham University Museums.

£75,000 was given in 1957 to build a Gulbenkian Wing at the Royal College of Art, London. A view of the Gulbenkian Lower Gallery with the recent exhibition *Design of the Times: One Hundred Years of the Royal College of Art*, 1996. Photo: RCA.

Oriental Studies at Durham University to help build the first wing of a Museum of Oriental Art and Archaeology, to be known as the 'Gulbenkian Museum'. The purpose matched the taste of the Founder, and until 1972, when the Foundation refocused its activities, support for archaeology was a minor, but consistent, part of its funding portfolio, with the Gulbenkian Archaeological series of monographs, begun in 1966 and published by Cambridge University Press, as its lasting monument. In November 1957 £75,000 was committed to a 'Gulbenkian Wing' for the Royal College of Art: an assembly hall, lecture room and exhibition space as part of the rebuilding of the College on its Kensington Gore site. When the hall was officially inaugurated on degree day in 1962, that year's Gold Medallist, David Hockney, graced the ceremony in a gold lamé suit.

A grant of £28,000 was made to the University of the West Indies in 1964 to meet the cost of building and equipping a Studio Block for its Centre for the Creative Arts. The Centre was formally opened in 1968 by HRH Princess Alice of Athlone, Chancellor of the University.
Photo: University of the West Indies.

The third award was less glamorous, but no less significant. £8,000 was given to help complete the Middlesbrough Little Theatre in Yorkshire, the first new theatre to be built since the war. Until the rise in costs in the early 1970s made it too expensive (and by which time the Arts Council's own building programme, Housing the Arts, launched in 1965, was in operation) the Foundation made a significant contribution to the construction of new theatres and arts centres. Early grants went to the new Mermaid Theatre in the City of London, the London Academy of Music and Drama and the new Nottingham Playhouse. There was money for refurbishments at the Oxford and Liverpool Playhouses, the Cheltenham Everyman and for the restoration of the Georgian Theatre Royal, Richmond, Yorkshire. Having already helped extend Aldeburgh's Jubilee Hall, when Benjamin Britten's Aldeburgh Festival expanded in 1967 the Foundation contributed to the new concert hall at Snape Maltings. The amateur Tredegar Thespian Players got £700, and the Questors in Ealing £8,000 towards realising their design for a flexible theatre space. As part of the United Kingdom Branch's responsibilities for the Commonwealth, Ibadan University received £3,000 towards completing its theatre in time for Nigeria's independence in 1960. The Theatre Guild of British Guiana (as Guyana was then) was given £500 for seating; in 1964 the University of the West Indies at Kingston Jamaica received £28,000 to begin building an arts centre.

The Bridges Report

The somewhat haphazard pattern of the first grant decisions shows that in the early days the United Kingdom Branch was still unsure of how it should proceed. The first step was to decide which areas should in principle be excluded so that the Branch's Director, Allen Sanderson, could be given the authority to turn them down – an important delegation of power that helped to build the self-reliance and responsibility of the Foundation's staff.

The second step was to ensure that the Trustees in Lisbon could be confident that their funds would be well spent promoting the arts in Britain. It was decided to seek out advice on how the Foundation's arts policy should be shaped, and in January 1958 Sanderson brought together a small committee of what can only be described as the very Great and the Good. The chairman was Lord Bridges, son of the Poet Laureate Robert Bridges, who had retired as Head of the Civil Service in 1956 and accepted a peerage. As Secretary to Churchill's wartime cabinet he had been the most important official in the land. He was Chairman of the Royal Fine Arts Commission and a Trustee of the Pilgrim Trust, which in 1940 had helped to create the Council for the Encouragement of Music and the Arts (CEMA). He was joined by Sir George Barnes, the founding Head of the BBC's Third Programme, and the Countess of Albemarle, formerly on the Arts Council, Chairman of the Ministry of Education's committee on the Youth Service, a Trustee of the Carnegie Trust who also served on the University Grants Committee and the Museums and Galleries Commission.

The fourth member was Noël Annan, Provost of King's College, Cambridge. Annan recalled in a letter to the Foundation in 1989:

> I was by far the least experienced of the committee. George Barnes knew a great deal from his time as Director of the BBC's Third Programme but the most dynamic member was Diana Albemarle who was enormously knowledge-able about local government and all sorts of voluntary organisations. She had already been made a Dame and no one was more appropriately dubbed. The gentle Secretary Allen Sanderson used occasionally to remind us after one of Diana's more forthright speeches that although the committee should give untrammelled advice it was for the Trustees as advised by their Secretary whether to receive it.

The administrative secretary to the Bridges Committee was George Christie, whose father John had founded Glyndebourne Opera before the war and who wanted him to learn about arts administration. When the 23-year-old George Christie joined the Foundation in 1957 he was 'green, unemployable and nervous' in his first salaried job. As he recorded in the 1994 *Annual Report*: 'I was given a secretary far more intelligent than myself and became more nervous . . . through [Sanderson's] spirit of generosity I gained the grains of self-respect.' Christie stayed with the Foundation until 1962, when he left to take over Glyndebourne following his father's death, and was replaced by Christopher Rye, who had been Director of Lincolnshire Arts Association.

Lord Bridges and his committee met regularly at the Foundation's offices at 3 Prince Albert Road, but also visited Bristol, Cardiff, Glasgow, Liverpool, Newcastle upon Tyne and Nottingham. There was a purpose to this, for when their report, *Help for the Arts*, was published on 18 June 1959 it was apparent that some of the wartime spirit of CEMA and the Pilgrim Trust had lingered on. In spite of their establishment status, the committee showed no metropolitan bias, for their main concern was that contact with the arts had significantly declined in the provinces since the war. Support for the arts in general seemed 'rather scrappy and patchy'. 'Far too few people seem to recognise the place which the arts should play in the life of the nation as a whole, or if they recognise it, show a marked reluctance to meet the cost.' There were other now familiar concerns: the rising costs of the arts, the need to foster experiment, the lack of space for the arts in the school curriculum, the need for private patronage to be encouraged by tax relief. More originally, there was concern about the 'passive' attitude of universities, and the needs of Britain's post-war New Towns.

With personal private patronage having almost disappeared, the Bridges Committee saw charitable trusts like the Gulbenkian taking over the role, and exercising their freedom from official constraints: 'If trusts will not back their fancy and be bold and be prepared to face ridicule, how can state patronage, which is accountable to public criticism, be expected to do anything more than play safe?' There was good advice on future policy and governance: 'It is the duty of a trust to encourage and foster new develop-ments or growing points, where there is a reasonable chance that the new development will later on either be self-supporting or will attract permanent support whether from public funds or from elsewhere.' But there was no need to support every new idea, and it was essential that its resources should not 'become, as it were, permanently mortgaged to the support of particular institutions or objects'. This has been a ruling principle of the United Kingdom Branch, where rarely will any project or activity be supported for more than five years, even if the recipient organisations themselves have a longer-term relationship with the Foundation.

In terms of policy, the committee urged the Foundation to concentrate on the provinces. For museums and galleries they proposed a network of strong centres not unlike the regional 'hubs' that began to be created with government support a mere half-century later following the Museums, Libraries and Archives Council's report *Renaissance in the Regions* of 2001. The Foundation could not try to build such a network itself, although it made grants to a number of area museums councils. Its vision for the arts was that the dozen largest cities would more fully recognise the contribution that culture could play in civic life, and to that end it suggested funding the appointment of arts officers to service regional consortia of local authorities – a proposal of long-term significance, as we shall see.

A trust 'should never forget', the committee refreshingly pointed out, 'that artists, and not institutions, create art'. Unlike the Arts Council it believed a trust should be prepared to back individuals. It had plenty of ground-breaking ideas, such as for the first artist-, poet- or playwright-in-residence schemes in Britain. It urged specific help for artists in mid-career, purchasing schemes, commissions, and support for exhibitions and the orchestral performance of new work. The committee was uncertain what to do about opera and ballet, but saw the need for a National Opera School (this was later to materialise as help for the London Opera Centre). Children's theatre also had potential: following earlier grants, the Unicorn Theatre for Children was to be helped acquire a lease on the Arts Theatre in London 1967. The committee was not worried by the new technology of entertainment, advocating film as an educational tool, and arguing that television would increase the appetite for live performance and raise audience expectations. The suggestion that the television companies might create their own acting troupes, however, fell on stony ground.

Above all, Lord Bridges's slim but elegant report argued that the Foundation should use its independence and not behave like the state or its surrogate, the Arts Council. It confirmed Whishaw and Sanderson's view that the arts should be the United Kingdom Branch's principal focus in the following years, and it was not until the early 1970s that the combined expenditure of the Education and Social Welfare Departments matched that of the Arts. *Help for the Arts* established a precedent and a pattern for the Foundation, so that when an issue arose that was believed to be important, in whatever field, a group of experts would be brought together, a report produced, and then a policy developed. In the arts it was the first of a series of important reports with which the Foundation has been associated, either as instigators or co-funders, that are milestones in the development of national cultural policy: Lord Redcliffe-Maud's *Support for the Arts in England and Wales* in 1976; Naseem Khan's *The Arts Britain Ignores* of the same year; Ken Robinson's *The Arts in Schools* in 1982; John Myerscough's *The Economic Importance of the Arts in Britain* in 1988; and François Matarasso's *Use or Ornament? The social impact of participation in the arts* in 1997.

Education and Social Welfare

In the other two fields to which the Foundation has made its principal commitment, Education and Social Welfare, the United Kingdom Branch was at first as tentative as it had been in the Arts. In the latter part of the 1950s the overwhelming majority of grants were responsive to a sense of general need, and widely varied: outings for deaf children, a youth club in Belfast, the Church of England Welfare Council and the Family Discussion Group for example. But there were a handful of grants that are significant in sign-posting the direction in which the Foundation was to develop.

Two grants – one to Voluntary Service Overseas and the other to the Samaritans – show a knack for choosing winners at an early stage. In both instances the Gulbenkian was backing people, not just projects. VSO was set up in 1958 by the educationist Alec Dickson, originally as a means of providing school leavers with an opportunity to serve deprived communities abroad. When Dickson left VSO in 1962 following a disagreement over policy, the Foundation kept faith with him, and gave him start-up funding to

The Rev. Chad Varah, founder of the Samaritans (which received grants from the Foundation in 1957 and 1961), and two helpers at their base in the Crypt of St Stephen Walbrook, London.
Photo: Northcliffe Newspapers Group Ltd.

found Community Service Volunteers, similar in principle to VSO, but directed to community work in Britain.

The Samaritans was the idea of the Anglican priest Chad Varah. He set up a confidential helpline, what he called 'a 999 for the suicidal', with a single telephone. At the time suicide was illegal, so many people who felt suicidal were unable to talk to anyone about it freely. The first call was received on 2 November 1953, and since then the organisation has grown to encompass 203 branches throughout the United Kingdom and the Republic of Ireland. Along the way tens of thousands of people have been helped, and society's attitude to suicide has changed.

In both cases, the Foundation was spotting 'social entrepreneurs' – those energetic and charismatic individuals who dedicate their talents to improving life for others – and the list of ventures that were given their start in life through Gulbenkian grants is both distinguished and remarkable. In addition to VSO and the Samaritans it includes the housing charity Shelter, the racial equality charity the Runnymede Trust, the National

Council for One Parent Families and the Coin Street Community initiative, a pioneering community-led building project on London's South Bank whose history is recorded fully in their book, *There is another way . . . Coin Street Community Builders: Social enterprise in action*. All of these would be unlikely to have come into being were it not for the money, and also the boost in confidence that accompanies hard cash, provided by the Gulbenkian. As Iain Tuckett, one of the founders of the initiative, told us, the keystone grant of £2,500 from the Foundation encouraged other funders, and persuaded the local authority to take them seriously. Paul Curno, later Deputy Director of the Foundation, describes the Coin Street initiative as 'an amazing example of community work, that offered a new model beyond the playgroup and tenants' associations, inspiring several hundred development trusts around the country'.

A Community Service Volunteer painting a mural at the Whittington Hospital, London, in the 1970s. Photo: Sally and Richard Greenhill, Photographers Photo Library.

Another early grant is significant in showing a method of working that was to become a feature of the Foundation's approach to problem-solving. As with the Bridges Committee, rather than simply providing money, the Foundation sought answers; it decided to enquire and report so that its decisions would be firmly based on the best available knowledge. The language of the following grant report from 1960 reflects the characteristic culture of the charitable world in those post-war days, but it also shows a fresh approach emerging through practice:

> The Foundation financed and published in 1959 an inquiry on 'The Needs of Youth in Stevenage' by a committee led by Brigadier E.T. Williams, CBE, DSO (Warden of Rhodes College, Oxford, and former Chief of Intelligence to Field Marshal Lord Montgomery) and including Mr Frankie Vaughan and others. The report emphasised that 'blokes are more important than bricks'. So before planning a central youth club for teenagers, the New Town decided to appoint as 'youth officer' Mr C. St John Ellis, a former master at Radley, who won the George Medal as an RNVR officer during the war and afterwards sailed his yacht *Theodor* to America and back with a crew of school-leavers.

Here we see the joining of the Great and the Good with those who had hands-on experience. Frankie Vaughan (described as 'a variety artiste', and who might be characterised as the Sting or Bono of his day) had come up the hard way in Liverpool and had poured his energy and money into helping others, particularly through Boys' Clubs. Initial ideas about how best to help in Stevenage were challenged, and after proper deliberation and expert testimony, the committee changed tack: the idea of a building was put to one side, and a youth officer was appointed instead. This sequence: engage, network, enquire, deliberate, act, was to be followed again and again by the Foundation over the years.

Building on Bridges: the Regional Arts Associations

From 1959 the Bridges Report gave a direction to the choice of arts projects to be supported. One grant was to prove as important for London as the provinces: in 1960 the new director of the Shakespeare Memorial Theatre was given £17,000 over three years to be able to put under contract an ensemble of actors who would appear both in London and Stratford. As he acknowledges in his autobiography, with the help of George Christie, Peter Hall had got the seed money to launch the Royal Shakespeare Company at the Aldwych. Further grants to the RSC were to follow.

The most important outcome of *Help for the Arts* was the Foundation's contribution to the creation of the Regional Arts Associations. When the

The Foundation gave the Shakespeare Memorial Theatre £17,000 in 1960 towards an ensemble of actors who would work in London and Stratford. Queen Margaret (Peggy Ashcroft) cursing Richard (Ian Holm) in a 1963 production of *Richard III* at the Royal Shakespeare Theatre, Stratford, directed by Peter Hall, John Barton and Frank Evans. Photo: Tom Holte Theatre Photographic Collection. © Shakespeare Birthplace Trust.

Arts Council closed one of its last surviving regional offices in Bristol in 1955, local enthusiasts decided to keep in being a federation of thirty arts centres across seven counties as the South Western Arts Association. Early in 1959 the Foundation gave the Association £8,000 over three years towards administration costs and activities. In 1960, in line with the Bridges Report, it decided to offer to pay two-thirds of the cost of employing an 'area arts officer' for a group of local authorities, if they would jointly find the rest. This was set up as a carrot to see if local authorities could be tempted to pick up the Bridges Report idea. The Foundation was thus ready to help when a group of local authorities formed the North Eastern Arts Association (later Northern Arts) in 1962. It continued to help as other Regional Arts Associations came on stream, up to the completion of the network with the South East Wales Arts Association in 1973, by which time there were eleven Regional Arts Associations in England, plus the Greater London Arts Association, and three in Wales. Each had a distinctive identity and slightly different constitutional arrangements; only Buckinghamshire stood aloof.

Since they had been formed partly to fill a gap left by the Arts Council, there was always a certain tension between the Regional Arts Associations and the metropolis, which complicated matters for the Foundation. RAAs were better disposed to amateur activities and what was to become known as community arts. As member organisations they were more democratic, with a mixture of funding sources including universities and business, as well as foundations and the Arts Council. The hope was that local authorities would channel their funds through the RAAs, and for a time there was parity between local authority and Arts Council funding, but as pressure on local government finance grew in the 1970s, the Arts Council became by far the biggest funder, so that by the 1990s more than 90 per cent of the finance came from London.

The debate about what was 'national' and what 'regional' was difficult to resolve, especially when larger organisations got funding from both their RAA and London. By 1975 the Arts Council was favouring the idea of 'devolution' – handing over the funding of organisations to the appropriate RAA – but its attempt in 1984 to solve the problems created by the imminent abolition of the Metropolitan County Councils with a devolution policy called *The Glory of the Garden* proved farcical. In 1989 devolution, or delegation as it was now known, of Arts Council clients to the regions was imposed by the government as a result of the Wilding Report, and the twelve Regional Arts Associations were tidied up into ten Regional Arts Boards. Delegation proved a slow process, and was still not complete when in 2001 the Arts Council of England (the Scottish and Welsh Arts Councils having been truly devolved in 1994) announced that it was abolishing the Regional Arts Boards and reintegrating the London and regional offices into a single system. Today, RAAs are no more, but for forty years the principles of the Bridges Report had helped shape the cultural landscape, and the 'provinces' are no longer the 'Third World of underdevelopment and depriva-tion in all the arts and crafts' that Lord Redcliffe-Maud discovered when he surveyed Britain for the Foundation in 1976.

From 'Charity' to 'Social Welfare'

In May 1961, the Foundation suffered a blow when Allen Sanderson unex-pectedly died, aged 48. Whishaw records that he consulted his advisers among the Great and the Good, and it was suggested that the 55-year-old, Cambridge-educated, James Thornton would be suitable. Thornton had joined the BBC in 1936 and risen to the senior administrative post of Deputy-Secretary of the Corporation. Whishaw writes, 'With that recom-mendation I looked no further', but he appears to have regretted the decision. 'He was a good administrator, but did not have Allen's flair, nor really the kind of experience we needed.' Thornton took an interest in archaeology (his wife was an archaeologist and had received a small grant from the Foundation in 1958) from which, as we have seen, the Foundation was later to withdraw. Under Thornton, in 1966, the title of Secretary to the Foundation was modernised to that of Director. Sadly, he too was to die in post, in 1969.

One of Thornton's first tasks was to complete the move into new offices at 98 Portland Place, not far from two other cultural institutions, the Royal Institute of British Architects and, further south, the BBC. Like their previous offices in Prince Albert Road, Portland Place was a Crown Property, a Nash Terrace that had been badly damaged by bombing during the war. This meant that the Foundation was able to organise the interiors how it wished, provided that the upper floors remained residential. Student accommodation was created for scholars arriving from Portugal and elsewhere on Gulbenkian grants, plus a flat for visiting Trustees and executives from Lisbon. As a canny lawyer, Whishaw was able to secure a sixty-year lease – without rent reviews – that continues to this day.

In 1960 the London Branch acquired a new recruit, Richard Mills, who was to stay at the Foundation until his retirement in 1980, by which time, according to Whishaw's successor as London Trustee, Mikhael Essayan, he had become 'the grand old boy of the social welfare world'. A Welshman, Mills's background was eclectic. He had worked as an insurance salesman and for the Iron and Steel Federation, but his main professional career had been in social services, broadly described, in Wales, in Bristol, and with what was later to become the National Council for Voluntary Organisations. His

The Greenhouse Trust was given a grant of £5,000 in 1966 for its work with 'unclubable boys', later extended to include girls. Photo: Clifford Shirley.

private tragedy was that his eldest son was born autistic at a time when there was very little help for parents of such children, which led him to help found the National Autistic Society. While living in the East End settlement, Cambridge House, he had come into contact with Peter Kuenstler, the Oxford academic who was to become an important adviser to the Foundation, and who in 1961 published a pioneering book, *Community Organisation in Great Britain*, that examined how communities could be helped to help themselves. The roots of the Gulbenkian's concern with issues of community can be traced to this connection.

Mills's knowledge of, and enthusiasm for, communal living and communal problem-solving began to show in his first five years in post with grants for the homeless and the rehabilitation of offenders, for example. This gradual shift in emphasis towards a focus on community work was formalised as policy in an internal review by Mills in 1964, where he discerned 'a major trend in social care in recent years ... away from institutional care and towards community care'. In a Foundation press release of 1965 the policy shift is made public: support for charity and social welfare will be concentrated on 'the development of community services' and on 'the resettlement in the community of three very different classes of person – former patients of mental hospitals, unmarried homeless mothers with

Red Road Flats, Glasgow, 1975, the highest tower blocks in Europe. From a collection of inner-city documentary photographs taken in the 1970s with funding from the Foundation. Photo: © Chris Steele-Perkins, Exit Photography Group project.

children, and discharged prisoners.' This is reinforced in the following year's annual press statement where, as Director, Thornton declares that 'the list of grants made to charitable and social work reveals the Foundation's particular interest in what is coming to be known as community work or community service. The training needed for social work is also a continuing concern of the Trustees.'

There is here a recognition that the infrastructure to support community work is vital – that there is little point in funding initiatives without a well-researched and articulated framework, that a conceptual grasp is needed to underpin practical ventures, and that those working in the field themselves need to develop. In other words, beneficial change happens through a marriage of thinking and doing. The Gulbenkian played an important role in forming, nurturing and reflecting the field of community: intellectually, through committees and their publications; structurally, through support to new umbrella bodies like the Community Development Foundation

The conditions experienced by some of Shelter's early clients. The Foundation supported the charity with £45,000 in 1969. Photo: Shelter.

launched in 1968; and practically, through support to radical initiatives such as a grant of £5,000 in 1966 towards a 'new experimental school for malad-justed children' and one of £2,250 to run a house with communal facilities for unmarried mothers in South-East London.

It is at this point, in the mid-1960s, that the new breed of community worker was being called upon to face a fresh set of societal problems, and was striving to find creative ways of dealing with those problems. Harold Wilson's Labour government came into power in 1964 promising a major programme of house building, but many people still lived in Victorian slums, while new tower blocks and estates were throwing up problems of their own, including vandalism, community breakdown and crime. The plight of the homeless was vividly illustrated in 1966 by Ken Loach's *Cathy Come Home*, a television drama that generated national anguish. Simultaneously, in fact almost to the day, the charity Shelter came into being, with Foundation support of £45,000 over three years.

Spurred on by public indignation and a new willingness to protest, legislators were beginning to turn their minds to tackling the legal and social inequalities between men and women, white and black, straight and gay. The Sixties' appetite for experimentation had its part to play. Communes might not be able to solve the housing crisis, but the activities of a few hippies and radical clerics at the margin made people think about the possibilities: why not try communal homes for the rehabilitation of offenders?

For those wishing to experiment, the notion of community was usefully vague. An unpublished Foundation policy paper by Richard Mills of January 1966 recognises that 'community' can become a catch-all: '''Community work", as may be expected, covers a number of projects . . . ranging from community associations to housing trusts, rehabilitation schemes for ex-mental patients, and the writing of a text-book.' The belief that people might achieve things together – that solutions would not come from the powers-that-be and the Establishment, but rather from self-help – was very much in the spirit of the times, but was not to become part of mainstream political thinking for another thirty years. Community work was opposed to the ideologies of both the Labour and Conservative Parties. Labour saw solutions coming from the state, while the Conservatives believed that individuals held the key to their own improvement. Neither saw the unruly demotic power of the people as particularly welcome.

The approach pioneered by the Gulbenkian rested on a belief that community solutions – people banding together rather than acting as individuals or through the organisations of the state – could tackle housing, their environment, the discrimination that they suffered as a group, and so on. This was a fundamentally different approach to that of traditional charity, and shows a deeply changed relationship between donor and recipient. Here, as in the case of the start-up of a family centre in the Sparkbrook area of Birmingham in 1964, the recipient is not a passive creature, but an empowered actor. The donor sees himself as acting in co-operation with the recipient, not as simply dispensing funds. In 1969, this change of direction was reflected in the language that the Gulbenkian now decided to adopt. In the annual press release the term 'charity' disappears, and is replaced forever afterwards by the phrase 'social welfare'.

Help to the Arts

Guided by the principles of the Bridges Report, the Foundation entered the Sixties willing and able to help contemporary artists. In the field of music, an early decision to subsidise the recording of contemporary classical music led to the launch of the 'Music Today' series with EMI in 1965. Benjamin Britten, Elizabeth Lutyens, Peter Maxwell Davies, Richard Rodney Bennett, Harrison Birtwistle and Pierre Boulez were among the composers to be featured. This scheme was continued with Argo in 1973. (In 2001 the Foundation returned to the practice of producing recordings when the Anglo-Portuguese Cultural Relations Programme released the first of a series of CDs, *Exploratory Music from Portugal*.)

Pierre Boulez conducting the BBC Symphony Orchestra in 1973 for a recording of Messiaen's *Poemes pour Mi*. The 'Music Today' series of records of outstanding modern music was made by EMI under the auspices of the Foundation between 1965 and 1968. The scheme was continued with Argo in 1973.

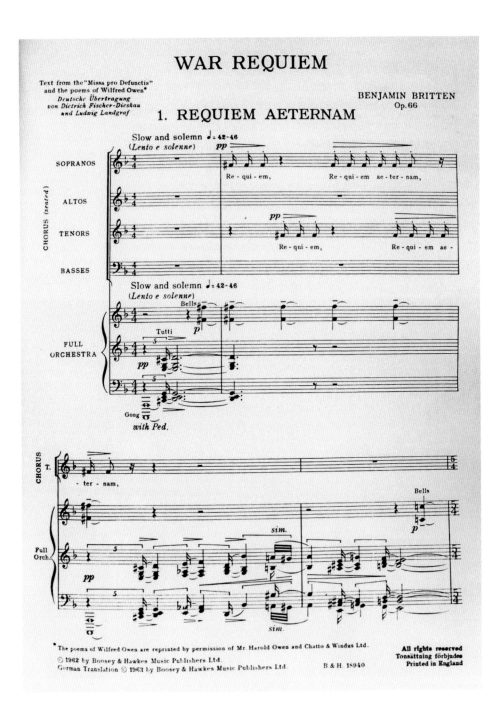

Benjamin Britten's *War Requiem* was commissioned to celebrate the consecration of the new Coventry Cathedral with the aid of a Foundation grant in 1961. © 1961 by Boosey & Hawkes Music Publishers. Reproduced by kind permission of Boosey & Hawkes Music Publishers Ltd.

In 1961 the Foundation helped the Northern Sinfonia in Newcastle become a full-time orchestra, and in 1963 this was followed by the Bristol Sinfonia. (While the Northern Sinfonia thrives, the Bristol Sinfonia went out of business in the 1980s.) A long association with the activities of Dartington Hall was begun when in 1960 a grant enabled the Dartington String Trio to become a Quartet. Harlow New Town Music Association received funds for a residency by the Alberni String Quartet. Concerts of new music were subsidised and in 1961 support was given to the performances celebrating the consecration of the new Coventry Cathedral, which included Britten's *War Requiem*. Young artists were subsidised at the Wigmore Hall and young audiences at Covent Garden. Liverpool's young music clubs, known locally as 'music boxes' were supported, as was the Rural Music Schools Association. In 1968 the Foundation's most important arts

The Rural Music Schools Association was given a grant of £13,500 in 1972 to introduce the Suzuki method of violin teaching in the UK. Photo: Jean Salder, Rural Music Schools Association.

63

grant was £50,000 to the Sadler's Wells Opera Company to help it transfer to the Coliseum in St Martin's Lane, where it became English National Opera.

In the same way that the Bridges Report had set out a general policy for funding the arts, music policy became more focused following the publication in September 1965 of *Making Musicians*, an investigation into the professional training of musicians chaired for the Foundation by Sir Gilmour Jenkins, a former Permanent Secretary, and Vice President of the Royal Academy of Music. This was the beginning of a long-standing commitment to training in the arts professions. The Foundation's Young Conductors scheme, which had started funding a trainee conductor at the Bournemouth Symphony Orchestra in 1962, was extended, and £5,000 given to the Yehudi Menuhin School in 1965, founded in 1963. Both Chetham's School in Manchester and Wells Cathedral School were similarly helped to become specialist schools for musically gifted children. One of the problems highlighted by *Making Musicians* was the difficulty music students at the London academies had in finding anywhere to live. In 1967 the Foundation put £125,000 into a partnership with the Henry Wood Memorial Fund to establish a hall of residence in South London, Henry Wood House. Not neglecting the individual, the first five Gulbenkian Foundation Music Fellowships were announced, with the intention of helping young professionals establish themselves as soloists. The pianist John Lill and the baritone Benjamin Luxon were among the first to benefit from a scheme that continued, with interruptions, till 1979. A commissioning fund for contemporary classical music was set up in 1968.

The Gulbenkian and the Tate: 54/64 and Beyond

In the field of the visual arts, help for individual painters and sculptors had begun in 1960, when a distinguished committee of artists, dealers and teachers, chaired by the doyen of British art education, Sir William Coldstream, was set up by the Foundation to advise on a fellowship scheme for older artists, and to choose each year two artists under 30 who would have two-thirds of their work bought by the Foundation, up to a limit of £500 (a significant sum in those days). The Foundation's Collection of

Modern British Art was officially established in 1968, but collecting had begun as far back as 1959 when £10,000 was awarded to the British Council to help its touring collection of contemporary work. The Council's exhibitions, especially at the Venice Biennale, had helped to establish international reputations for British artists such as Henry Moore, and it had started to collect in 1946. Now it was also able to buy works on behalf of the

British paintings from the Centro de Arte Moderna José de Azeredo Perdigão, Lisbon, shown in the 1997 *Treasure Island* exhibition (this page and overleaf).

Patrick Caulfield, *View of the Bay*, 1964). Oil on board, 122 x 183 cm. © The Estate of Patrick Caulfield 2005. All Rights Reserved, DACS. Photo: MACJAP.

Howard Hodgkin, *Mr and Mrs Patrick Caulfield*, 1969/70. Oil on canvas, 107 x 127 cm. Courtesy of the artist. Photo: MACJAP.

David Hockney,
Renaissance Head,
1963. Oil on canvas,
122 x 122 cm.
© David Hockney.
Photo: MACJAP.

Gulbenkian, and tour them for a number of years before they reverted to the Foundation. A further award of £10,000 was made in 1963, helping the British Council expand its commitment to contemporary British artists, and the Collection is particularly strong in its holdings of the leading artists of the Sixties. Purchases for the Foundation's Modern British Art Collection had to be suspended in 1972 when finances became tight but restarted in 1985, and acquisitions have continued. Since the Foundation's Centro de Arte Moderna José de Azeredo Perdigão opened in Lisbon in 1983 the Collection has been held there, constituting one of the largest collections of contemporary British art outside the United Kingdom. The Collection is surveyed in *Treasure Island*, the catalogue for an adventurous exhibition at the Centro de Arte Moderna in 1997, curated by its present Director, Jorge Molder.

In the 1960s the Foundation also ran a scheme to help local regional art galleries acquire contemporary British works, besides contributing to the costs of new buildings or galleries. The Herbert Art Gallery in Coventry, the Penwith Society of Art in St Ives, the Midland Group in Nottingham, the Bear Lane Gallery and the Museum of Modern Art in Oxford, the Kirkwall Arts Centre in Orkney and the Arnolfini in Bristol were all helped. Uganda acquired its first permanent art gallery with the help of a grant of £8,500 to Makere University, Kampala, in 1966.

The Foundation's highest-profile contribution in the field of the visual arts was to mount an exhibition at the Tate Gallery in 1964. The idea originated in the United Kingdom Branch's arts advisory committee, where the principal of Chelsea School of Art, Lawrence Gowing, who was also a trustee of the Tate, had taken over chairmanship of the purchasing committee from Coldstream. Covering the years 1954 to 1964, this was to be the first major international survey of contemporary art ever held at the Tate, and the first such show to be mounted in Britain since Roger Fry's *Second Post-Impressionist Exhibition* in 1912, which provided the model.

The organisation was entirely the Gulbenkian's, which committed an initial £35,000. Gowing worked with his friend Alan Bowness, then teaching at the Courtauld Institute, and with Philip James from the Arts Council, who had long experience of mounting ACGB exhibitions. With an installation designed by Peter and Alison Smithson and a catalogue laid out by the leading typographer Edward Wright, *54/64: Painting and Sculpture of a*

Arnolfini, Bristol, received £20,000 in 1973 towards equipping the new arts centre in a converted warehouse. Photo: Arnolfini.

Ulster Museum, Belfast, received £1,500 from the Regional Galleries Purchase Fund towards Anthony Caro's sculpture *Rainy Day*, 1971. Welded steel, painted brown, 488 x 658 x 889 cm. © Barford Sculptures Ltd. Collection: Ulster Museum, Belfast.

Decade struck a new note of modernity as it took over the central, Duveen Galleries of a still very traditional Tate. There were 367 works by 169 artists in the loan exhibition (with very few works from the Tate or other British public collections, a reflection of acquisition policies of the period). Starting with Matisse, Picasso, Braque and Kokoschka (all alive and working in 1954) the show brought together the American Abstract Expressionist and Colour Field painters, the English Constructivists and 'Situation' artists, European Art Brut and Abstractionists, and American and British Pop artists. The last to figure in the exhibition were David Hockney and Allen Jones.

Partly because the show demonstrated that European contemporary art could stand up to the all-conquering cultural energy and wealth of the Americans, *54/64* had a shaping influence on public taste. The work of at least twenty artists in the show entered public collections, including the Gulbenkian's. Sir Nicholas Serota, Director of the now vastly expanded Tate, acknowledges the show as a key moment in the formation of his own interest in modern art. The spirit of the exhibition was summed up in the unsigned catalogue introduction:

World wars have left more of a mark on twentieth-century art and its development than we are usually prepared to admit. Only in the middle Fifties was it
possible to forget them: no longer was there a sense of living in a pre-war or a
post-war age .... the climate is once more favourable to art.

Ninety-five thousand people visited the exhibition between April and
June, a large number for those days, and a version of the show travelled to
America. But there had been tensions behind the scenes. According to
Frances Spalding's history of the Tate: 'Gowing had grossly overrun the
estimated expenditure and had done so in an overbearing, high-handed way
without expressing any regrets. Moreover, when asked for an explanation, he
had attempted to cast blame on the staff of the Foundation.' Gowing had
'ruthlessly' cut Philip James out of the selection process, and in 1964 the
Foundation had to produce another £30,000, nearly doubling its original

Work shown at the exhibition *54/64: Painting and Sculpture of a Decade* (this page and overleaf).

Peter Lanyon, *Offshore*, 1959. Oil, 152 x 183 cm. © Sheila Lanyon. Photo: Birmingham Museums & Art Gallery.

commitment, although this was partly to subsidise the price of the catalogue. It was unfortunate for Gowing then, that at this very time he should be applying for the post of Director of the Tate. The chairman of the selection panel was none other than Lord Bridges, who took a dim view of what had gone on. Gowing did not get the job.

Relations with the Tate, however, did not suffer. In 1969, to mark the

Frank Auerbach, *Half-length of E.O.W. nude*, 1957. Oil, 76 x 51 cm.
© the artist.

centenary of Calouste Sarkis Gulbenkian's birth, the Foundation made its largest award in Britain to date, £250,000 towards the cost of building new galleries in the north-west quadrant of the Gallery. Whishaw recalled that he had been able to finance the grant 'without having to dip into our normal budget, because our funds were allocated in dollars and it was at the time of the devaluation in sterling, when Wilson's "pound in your pocket" statement was treated with ridicule . . . we had a bonus of more sterling for the dollars allocated.' The new galleries finally opened in 1979, and served as the principal space for temporary exhibitions at Millbank until the beginning of

The Tate Gallery extension in progress, October 1974. To commemorate the centenary of the birth of Calouste Sarkis Gulbenkian, a grant of £250,000 was made to the Tate in 1969 for the construction of galleries to house temporary exhibitions. Photo: Tate Archive 2006.

the twenty-first century. It is a sign of the inflation of art prices that in 2002 the cost to the Foundation of helping the Tate acquire the Portuguese-born Paula Rego's triptych *After Hogarth: Betrothal; Lessons; Wreck* was £50,000. In celebration of the long association with the Tate, and to mark the Foundation's 50th anniversary, in 2004 the first instalment of another exceptional grant was made in support of the recurrent exhibition of the latest work by contemporary artists, the *Tate Triennial 2006*, to be accompanied by a selection from the Foundation's own collection of Modern British Art.

Community Work and Social Change: the Younghusband Report

It is no coincidence that the United Kingdom Branch should have dropped the patronising language of 'charity' in favour of the more empowering concept 'social welfare' in 1969, for this was a pivotal time for social policy, as the forces of generational and political change created an extraordinary climate of private hedonism and public protest. On cue, the Foundation produced the highly influential Younghusband Report, *Community Work and Social Change*.

Born in 1902, Dame Eileen Younghusband had become a pioneer in social work, dedicating her life not only to the direct service of others, but to establishing social work as a professional field through writing about it and helping to create an infrastructure. She was a member of, and had chaired, numerous committees, both charitable and governmental. The Gulbenkian had chosen their chairman well. With a rigorous and studious mind, earnest, serious, caring, and determined to get things done, Younghusband was respected by government and practitioners; she continued to serve the Gulbenkian through the next decade, acting as a member of the Boyle, Serota and Jones Committees that advanced the work of her own.

The Younghusband Committee consisted of thirteen members, of whom eleven were academics. The other two were the highly regarded field worker Muriel Smith (whose original idea it was that the Gulbenkian should undertake this study), and Elizabeth Littlejohn, of the National Council for Voluntary Organisations. Their working methods helped ensure the eventual impact of the report. They used their networks and consulted widely, so that their conclusions were based on the most current practice. They also worked closely with the government's Seebohm Committee, which was meeting in parallel to produce a report on the future of the social services in Britain. Debate within the committee centred on what was the true nature of community work. According to the sociologist David Thomas:

> The educationalists argued that community work was an informal process in
> adult education, and that its values were in conflict with the statutory functions
> of social work which some members of the group viewed as controlling, manip-
> ulative and dependency-creating. The social work camp drew heavily on the
> integration of community work in American social work, could point at the
> general direction in which they knew the Seebohm Committee was heading
> and to the proposed new social services departments as obvious places in
> which to employ specialist community workers.

Although the Foundation's Younghusband Report did not resolve this issue, it was important in giving a seal of approval and respectability to community work, and the values it represented: 'The essence of community is a sense of common bond, the sharing of an identity, membership in a group holding some things, physical or spiritual, in common esteem, coupled with the acknowledgement of rights and obligations with reference to others so identified.' It was something of a coming of age for those who had been struggling to gain proper recognition for the last decade. According to Thomas, 'The Younghusband Report was one of the first to legitimate community work in Britain.'

The Foundation's release of the report helped to shape an environment where community work was being taken ever more seriously. Also in 1968, the government launched the Urban Aid Programme and the Community Development Programme. With Foundation help, the Young Volunteer Force Foundation, which was to become the Community Development Foundation, was established. The Association of Community Workers was formed and the Race Relations Act was passed. At least six Whitehall departments produced reports, legislation or administrative change that in one form or other showed the influence of 'community thinking'.

In 1969, George Goetschius's highly influential book *Working with Community Groups* was published; following the Skeffington Report, *People and Planning*, the Department of the Environment introduced new participatory procedures; while the Aves Report, *The Voluntary Worker in the Social Services*, recommended ways of encouraging members of the community to volunteer. The Redcliffe-Maud Royal Commission on Local Government in 1969 and the Local Authority Social Services Act of 1970 were early examples of 'joined-up' government that attempted to integrate social services at a local level. The Russell and Alexander Committees on adult education published their findings in 1973, and the Department of Health

In 1970, Northumberland and Tyneside Council of Social Service was awarded £12,000 over three years for the appointment of a community worker in the Byker area of Newcastle, which was undergoing redevelopment. Photo: NTCSS.

made public its own proposals for more community involvement in the National Health Service. The profound shift in the perception of community work that is shown in these examples must have been a source of quiet satisfaction in Portland Place.

A Policy for the Arts: the Government Catches Up

In spite of the social distress and educational needs that had to be addressed by the Foundation, the claim in the catalogue for *54/64* that 'the climate is once more favourable to art' felt justified as the Sixties reached their apogee. When Harold Wilson became Prime Minister in 1964, he decided to shift responsibility for government funding for the arts away from the tight-pursed Treasury to the Department for Education and Science, where the energetic Jennie Lee, widow of Aneurin Bevan, became Britain's first Minister for the Arts. In February 1965 she published a White Paper, *A Policy for the Arts*, the first time the government officially had one. The White Paper followed the Bridges Report in acknowledging that support so far had been modest and incoherent. It also followed Bridges in wanting to see more help to individual artists, and praised the development of Regional Arts Associations. More importantly, it announced that the Arts Council would have a new fund specifically for housing the arts, and that its grant-in-aid would be substantially increased. By 1970, when Labour lost power to the Conservatives, the ACGB grant-in-aid stood at £9.3 million.

The publication of the White Paper in 1965 coincided with a refinement in the Foundation's arts policy, as part of a general policy review driven by the needs of the Social Welfare and Education Departments. While the report *Making Musicians* concentrated efforts on professional musical training, as has been described, it was decided to focus on stimulating the enjoyment of the arts in the universities, whose passivity towards the performing arts had been noted in the Bridges Report. The government's decision to create six new universities following the Robbins Report of 1963, with their associated new campuses, together with the general expansion of the university and polytechnic sector, was an opportunity to create facilities whose amenities would be enjoyed, as the 1966 *Annual Report* put it,

Theatre Gwynedd, University College of North Wales, Bangor. The Foundation gave £25,000 in 1966 towards the cost of building the theatre, and a further £15,000 in 1969. Photo: Courtesy of National Museums Liverpool (Merseyside Maritime Museum).

'beyond the confines of the universities and also benefit those living in the city or district in which the university is situated'. Accordingly nearly half the Arts budget was committed to building mainly studio theatres on university campuses: Aberystwyth, Bangor, Coleraine, Edinburgh, Essex, Exeter, Hull, Kent, Newcastle, Stirling, Sussex, and Warwick all benefited. Whishaw shows his dry wit in recalling the opening ceremony of the Gulbenkian Theatre at the University of Kent: 'A considerable stir was caused, not by the beauty or otherwise of the theatre, but by the appearance standing at the front of the stage of a young man stark naked and full frontal.'

Alexander Dunbar

On the 1 January 1970 the Foundation welcomed a new Director, following the death of Jim Thornton. This time the post was advertised, but 40-year-old Scots-born Alexander Dunbar was no stranger, for he had been the first arts officer at the North Eastern Association for the Arts, and had risen to become Director when it became Northern Arts in 1967. He did not stay long at the Foundation, returning to Scotland in 1971 to become Director of the Scottish Arts Council. Dunbar decided to shift the buildings policy away from universities towards arts centres, theatres and art galleries, and instituted a special arts building fund of £125,000 for the purpose. He also launched a new policy for dance, which will be discussed in chapter three.

By 1970 the Foundation was operating in a completely different economic and cultural environment to 1956. The expansionist mood of the Sixties did not outlast the decade, and it was evident that the cost of building was rising faster than the Foundation's resources. But in its first fifteen years it had helped to change the climate for the arts from the tweedy seriousness of the 1950s to the more open and colourful optimism of the 1960s and, in its ambition to spread the enjoyment of the arts beyond the metropolis and the élite, it had made a contribution that remains in place. By the time it withdrew from its buildings programme altogether in the mid-1970s, the Foundation had spent £1 million on Britain's cultural bricks and mortar, worth at least twenty times that today.

In terms of social welfare and education, the Foundation had become a key player, capable of reshaping attitudes and policies. Richard Mills later said of the Younghusband Report that it had opened up 'a continent of opportunities for initiatory and innovatory action' for the Foundation. As this chapter ends, in 1972, that continent was about to be explored further, and new vistas opened, by the publication of the Boyle Report. At the same time, the arrival of a new Director, Peter Brinson, began a period when the three strands of the Branch's activities were to be woven together in the service of 'the common bond' of community.

CHAPTER 3

Building community

1972–1982

'We want to act where government does not act.'

PETER BRINSON, *ANNUAL REPORT* 1974

The linking theme of this chapter is the idea of Community, which became the watchword of the new Director, Peter Brinson. In a decade characterised by social unease and rampant inflation, the United Kingdom Branch encouraged people to find ways in which they could act for themselves. Inner-city deprivation, unemployment and race relations came to the fore, while in the field of the arts the Foundation played a leading role in supporting contemporary dance and the arts in education.

OPPOSITE: **Protest, Liverpool 8, 1975.** From a photographic study of inner-city areas undertaken with support from the Foundation. Photo: © Paul Trevor, Exit Photography Group project.

According to the Foundation's present Director, Paula Ridley, 'The 1960s were the glory days. Because of the massive expenditure the Gulbenkian was always up for something new.' In the 1970s, however, the Foundation was forced to take stock of its position. There were social, economic and political changes that called for a review of its internal structures; a new approach to policy was needed that would reflect the change in the landscape brought about by the growth of state funding both for the arts and social welfare, while the inflation of the 1970s significantly reduced the United Kingdom Branch's financial power. If the Branch gave a grant of £1,000 in 1970, to offer an equivalent amount in real terms in 1982 would have needed £4,389. But in spite of the continuing support of the Trustees in Lisbon, the total money available for grants over the same period went up not by 439 per cent, but only 172 per cent, from £660,527 in 1970 to £1,135,760 in 1982.

In 1975 'fighting deprivation and squalor in disadvantaged areas was a continuing concern of all three of the Foundation's Programmes'. National Union of Students, Student Community Action. Photo: Scanus, Brixton.

The process of reorganisation had begun under the short directorship of Alexander Dunbar in 1970 and 1971, but it was his successor, Peter Brinson, who was to give the Foundation's United Kingdom policies a new shape and purpose. 'We want to act where government does not act' was his watchword. By the time he took up his post in January 1972 much of the expansionist mood of the 1960s had evaporated. In 1970 the Conservatives, led by Edward Heath, unexpectedly defeated Labour, but they proved incapable of solving the country's deepening problems of inflation, recession and unemployment, and the wider sense of uncertainty and unease that these brought. The government's attempts to control wages and prices met resistance from a work force determined to defeat its industrial relations legislation, and the domestic atmosphere was further soured by racial tensions and the situation in Northern Ireland. To make matters worse, the Arab-Israeli war of 1973 provoked a rise in oil prices that contributed to a world recession.

When Labour scraped back into power in 1974 it proved no more capable of dealing with inflation or unemployment than the Conservatives. In 1974, with inflation at 24 per cent, the Foundation's *Annual Report* warned:

> Inflation in the arts probably runs at a rate half as high again as the national figure, due to the labour-intensive nature of most of the activities involved. Consequently, the size of the Branch's arts budget in real financial terms has been halved since 1967, a fact not appreciated by many applicants.

In the Autumn of 1976 the Labour government, in spite of having already made cuts that affected its spending on the arts, education and social welfare, was forced to reduce expenditure even further in order to secure a loan from the International Monetary Fund. In 1977 unemployment reached 1.4 million and Labour had to enter into a pact with the Liberals to stay in power. Unable to impose its wages policy on an increasingly recalcitrant country, Labour struggled on through the winter of discontent of 1978–9 until the failure of its proposals for devolved government in Scotland and Wales triggered the general election that brought Mrs Thatcher and a new brand of Conservatism to power.

Britain was not the only country to experience social and political upheaval. In 1974 the successes of the long-standing liberation movements in Portugal's African colonies produced revolution at home. The Gulbenkian had made a vital contribution to the social and cultural welfare of Portugal. As Ben Whitaker, who was to become a Director of the United Kingdom Branch, wrote of this period in his study, *The Foundations*:

> The Gulbenkian Foundation accounted for a larger proportion of the Portuguese economy than all the American foundations do in the US; it used to play an increasingly crucial part in a number of facets of Portuguese society, partly because the Portuguese government – unlike other ones – had not taken over the support of services the Foundation has pioneered.

The Foundation had also enabled many of the country's élite to study in Britain, providing them with the social centre and the support they needed at Portland Place, while it was not uncommon for Gulbenkian Trustees to move in and out of Portuguese government positions, as they still do.

The Gulbenkian was part of the public face of Portugal, and as such it could not avoid being at least partly identified with the old regime. As Sir Charles Whishaw has recorded, in 1974:

> The revolution in Portugal, the first of several and the most left wing, created problems for the Foundation as it did for individuals and corporations alike. Personal property was taken over, whether land, houses or shares; and 'people power' became common. Pressure within the Foundation – strikes threatened and actual – resulted in the departure of two members of the Board and workers' committees were formed whose aim was to control the grant decisions.

The Board in Lisbon went through difficult times in the mid-1970s, and the need to secure the Foundation's position meant that the United Kingdom Branch was left more to its own devices than it might otherwise have been. But, as Whishaw continues: 'Perdigão managed to ride out the internal problems with considerable diplomatic skill and it was to my great surprise that the ousted members of the Board returned some while later when the political scene had improved and the succession of governments moved a little to the right again.'

Rethinking the United Kingdom Branch

With so much change in the air, Peter Brinson's arrival in January 1972 was timely. Not unusually for people joining the Foundation, he was familiar with its workings, for in 1963 he had secured a grant of £9,850 towards setting up the Royal Ballet's 'Ballet for All' scheme, an outreach programme that toured the country with a group of young dancers in order to introduce audiences to the classical repertoire. Dance, both contemporary and classical, was Brinson's passion, but that did not prevent him giving his energies to everything else as well. His Deputy Director, Richard Mills, wrote in the 1995 *Annual Report*, following Brinson's death in 1995:

> He will be remembered as an incurable workaholic. He never seemed to stop working. There is no proof that he ever slept; and he seemed to subsist on a diet consisting of little else than white wine and the occasional apple. Most days he

would be working at the Foundation till late evening before leaving for a mysterious night life, about which we at Portland Place knew nothing, except that – Peter being Peter – it must all feed back, in one way or another, into his total commitment to human betterment.

Millicent Bowerman, who joined the United Kingdom Branch in 1978, told us that Brinson was in the office even on Christmas Day. 'He was tall, but slight, shy and immensely courteous, and strongly left-wing. He never talked to you from his desk, but got up and sat by a low coffee table, giving you his full attention.' Brinson was an aesthete but also a radical, and had been briefly imprisoned for his activities in support of the Campaign for

Patrick Harding-Irmer (top) and Darshan Bhuller (bottom) in Robert Cohan's *Hunter of Angels*, recorded on video in 1983, with support from the Foundation, in an experimental archiving project by the National Resource Centre for Dance, University of Surrey and London Contemporary Dance Theatre.
Photo: © NRCD.
Used with Permission.

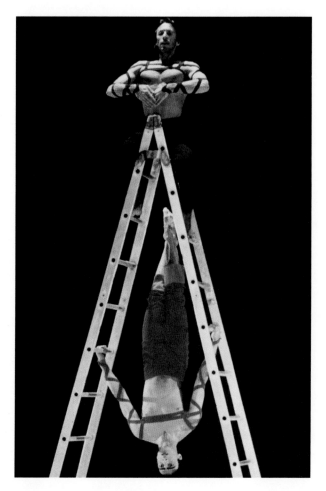

Nuclear Disarmament. Born in 1923, as a young man Brinson served as a tank commander in the Western Desert, and was injured as a paratrooper, before completing his studies at Oxford after the war. Film was his first interest before dance took over; as a freelance journalist he wrote for *The Times* on dance and *The Sunday Times* on wine, and in 1963, in collaboration with Peggy van Praag, he published his best-known book, *The Choreographic Art*. After four years running Ballet for All, in 1968 he was appointed Director of the Royal Academy of Dancing, but left after eighteen months, frustrated in his attempts to introduce administrative reform.

As an old friend of the Foundation, Brinson had been asked by Alexander Dunbar to advise on a new policy for dance. This led to the creation in 1971 of a dance advisory panel chaired by Brinson to oversee a £50,000 dance development fund. When Dunbar decided to move on later that year, Brinson was ready to take up the directorship. Whishaw had decided that it was time for a thorough reorganisation of the United Kingdom Branch and that Brinson was the man to do it.

Brinson's approach was two-fold. Firstly he wanted to give the Foundation a new public face through its publications. The *Annual Report* became an illustrated, informative account of the Foundation's activities that served as a commentary on the development of Foundation policies and acted as a guide to applicants. In his analysis of the United Kingdom Branch's Social Welfare programmes David Thomas has commented: 'Few foundations issued annual reports in the period under study, and none that did produced reports as informative and accessible.' In addition there were printed reports from working parties and Gulbenkian-sponsored conferences, as well as commissioned books. In 1978 Millicent Bowerman was brought in as Literary Editor to oversee a much more active publications programme. Bowerman, born in 1934, and a concert pianist, had been Deputy Director of the Greater London Arts Association, and in 1975 had gone to Ireland for the Foundation to research a report on the minimal provision that then existed for the arts. Bowerman worked for the Foundation until her retirement in 1994, also serving as Information Officer. She told us that most publications made a loss, 'but because our grants were tiny, the influence of putting what we had learned in a book could be enormous; there was no reference to cost whatsoever.' For a long time she was the only person with a computer – and the only female with her own office. Bowerman's publications programme was initially funded through a grant of £25,800 for three years; since then, the Branch's commitment to publishing has grown significantly so that it is now a notable feature of its work. Although the commissioned report has become a less viable way of influencing government since the rise of think-tanks such as Demos and the Institute for Public Policy Research (IPPR), the Foundation has become a niche publisher in its own right.

Brinson intended his policy to 'rouse and inform': Gulbenkian staff were encouraged to speak at seminars and conferences, and the offices at Portland Place were made available for meetings of interested parties. Most charities feel it inappropriate to spend money on entertaining, but Brinson saw the value in making people – especially those ministers and officials the Foundation wished to influence – feel comfortable. The basement canteen was turned into a restaurant with waiters and waitresses, and Brinson's knowledge of wine ensured that the Foundation kept a good table that was also an effective forum. The Labour Home Secretary Roy Jenkins would come to a discussion on race relations, Conservative Arts Minister Norman St John Stevas to talk about culture. The Great and the Good were not the sole beneficiaries, for everyone who came to Portland Place was given the same hospitality. Much later this included a homeless man who took up residence in nearby Park Crescent, and it became customary to take him lunch on a tray.

Peter Stark, a former Director of Northern Arts, recalls Brinson as:

> a warm and intelligent radical living in splendour in Portland Place and taking a
> real interest in us and what we were doing and groping towards. To come to
> London and visit the Foundation probably did more for our self-confidence than
> any number of Arts Council committees or grants. In retrospect it was also a
> gentle and caring education of future leaders or innovators delivered without
> too many of us noticing it.

Brinson believed in people, not projects; he liked, as he said, 'to go pontoon' on someone, meaning that he had more faith in the personalities behind a project than how it was written up.

Brinson's personal charm and the Foundation's hospitality ensured that he was able to create the partnerships and alliances that were necessary for the Gulbenkian to have an influence beyond its financial reach as a middle-scale grant-giver. In 1975 for instance the Community Councils

Development Group was joint-funded with the Joseph Rowntree Memorial Trust, and Newham Education Concern with the Sainsbury Family Trusts. As Richard Mills commented in his 'Reminiscences':

> More and more often the Branch found itself unable to assist some outstanding project except on the basis of joint funding with another source. Thus it became more important than ever to keep in touch with colleagues in other trusts with similar concerns.

In the Seventies at least 50 per cent of the Foundation's grants were given in co-operation with other sources of funding.

The other half of Brinson's policy was to bring the activities of the Arts, Education and Social Welfare Departments much closer together, and to rationalise their operations. Gradually the Arts Council model of regular advisory panels was abandoned in favour of *ad hoc* committees of experts brought together for specific tasks. Dunbar's decision to withdraw from large-scale building projects was followed by the letting-go of archaeology. In 1972 Anthony Wraight succeeded Christopher Rye as Assistant Director in charge of the Arts Programme. Short, bearded, very conscientious but somewhat abrasive, Wraight had served four years in prison for espionage on behalf of the Russians, a problem that Brinson treated with sympathy. Wraight stayed until 1977, leaving to become Drama Director for the Scottish Arts Council, when he was succeeded by Ian Lancaster, who had been working at the East Midlands Arts Association.

In 1974 Brinson took over the Education Programme in a reorganisation that led to the redundancy of Betty Hyams, who, as we have seen, had joined the Foundation in 1956 as Allen Sanderson's personal assistant, becoming an Assistant Director responsible for Education, Science and Archaeology ten years later. Under Dunbar an Education advisory panel had been set up in parallel to the successors of the committee that had produced the Bridges Report. Noël Annan, who had served on the Arts panel till 1964, returned in 1971 to become chairman of the Education panel, but there was evidently a lack of sympathy between Brinson and the sort of advisers he had inherited. Annan wrote later:

> The grants were being given increasingly to fringe activities such as street theatre, very much in the spirit of the early Seventies. What Mr Gulbenkian

would have thought of this is a matter for speculation. Kenneth Clark thought that he would have been outraged as in his view art meant high art, and quite a number of ventures which the Foundation was supporting were more political than artistic. Such at any rate was the view the committee took.

In 1973 the Education panel was merged with the Arts panel into a General Advisory Committee, which in 1976 was done away with altogether. One member, Lord Feversham, at that time chair of the Standing Conference of Regional Arts Associations, recalled: 'Following the revolution in Portugal the entire committee was disbanded – the reason given (although there may have been another one) that the London committees were, for want of a better term, too right-wing! However, I enjoyed the farewell dinner at the Connaught.'

Community Development and the Search for a Centre

As we saw in chapter two, the theme of 'community', as articulated in the Younghusband Report of 1968, had become the key to the Foundation's approach to social welfare. Brinson used it to bring the United Kingdom Branch's Departments much closer together, focusing all three on community relations, community action and community arts. As Richard Mills recalled: 'Throughout his time all three Programmes moved as one'. In Education and Social Welfare, assistance was primarily given to support self-help among people directly affected by deprivation or disadvantage of one sort or another. A second strand of grants supported those agencies and organisations that sought to promote and assist such self-help. This involved influencing policy, initiating training opportunities and disseminating infor-mation and learning, but one main focus was to try to create a national centre for community support.

The Social Welfare Programme, guided by the principles of the Younghusband Report, was further developed by the recommendations of a committee set up by the Foundation in 1969 under the chairmanship of Lord Boyle, Vice-Chancellor of Leeds University, and a former Minister of Education in the Macmillan government. The committee, seventy-member

The Community Work Group, 1970–3, chaired by Lord Boyle (centre), with Peter Brinson, Director of the Foundation's UK Branch (left), and Dame Eileen Younghusband. The Boyle Report, *Current Issues in Community Work*, was published on behalf of the Foundation by Routledge and Kegan Paul in 1973. Photo: Alan Cunliffe.

strong, was intended to act as a broad forum to promote the idea of community development. When it reported in 1973, the recommendations of *Current Issues in Community Work* were that the Foundation should establish both national and local forums and resource centres. The idea of local resource centres sprang from a concern about the growing profession-alisation of community work. There was a feeling that, as training and unionisation increased, homogenisation followed, destroying the free-flowing inter-disciplinarity that had characterised community work in the 1960s. In addition, it was felt that communities were suspicious of local authority 'community workers' and wanted resources of their own – partic-ularly places to meet. As Boyle Committee member Professor George Wedell recalled, 'Instead of promoting the further development of community work as a profession concerned with direct intervention, the committee looked at how these new community groups could be helped to be more effective.'

Not everyone agreed. Two members of the committee, Elisabeth Littlejohn, later Director of Community Work at the National Council for Voluntary Organisations, and sociologist Professor Robert Leaper saw the Boyle Committee as being too large to be effective, with a chairman who was too busy to devote enough time to it. But their main objection lay in the shift from supporting professionals to helping 'the community'. There are overtones of Annan's criticism of arts and education policy in Elisabeth Littlejohn's comment: 'Serious consideration of the theory and practice of community work . . . was swamped by a growing tide of quasi-political community action.'

Even before the Boyle Report had been published, its recommendations were being taken up by a new 'working group' chaired by Baroness Serota, the social reformer and deputy leader of the House of Lords. Her experience lay mainly in health and social security – she had been Minister of State under Richard Crossman. When she died in 2002 *The Guardian* wrote: 'Bea Serota was not the sort of politician who made headlines; she was the sort who got on with the job.' The Serota Committee was specifically tasked to look into the question of resources for community work and the proposal to establish community forums. Whereas the Younghusband and Boyle Committees had been invited to inquire and to recommend, the Serota Committee was set up in 1973 to take action – to turn proposals for national and local community resource centres into reality. It was charged with consulting about the proposals, and finding sources of funding to make them happen. As David Thomas has commented, the Serota Committee became 'in effect an executive arm of the Gulbenkian Foundation'.

Government backing for the Serota Committee's ideas was to prove elusive as civil service hostility combined with a general lack of enthusiasm, particularly among local authorities. It must have been dispiriting for Brinson to receive letters such as this in July 1974, from J. Gibson Kerr, Clerk to the Scottish Royal Burghs: 'Dear Mr Brinson, As you will appreciate, Local Authorities in Scotland are extremely busy meantime, and it is difficult to get any response . . .'

Nor was the voluntary sector united on the issue, and subtle man-oeuvring by those in opposition meant that when the proposal for a national resource centre and regional forums was formally put to Lord Windlesham, the Minister responsible in 1975, it was turned down. From the government's point of view it may have seemed that all of the things being proposed were already covered. They were funding Community Service Volunteers and the new Volunteer Centre, and the Home Office had commissioned a review of the Community Development Foundation. As we have seen, the CDF had started life in 1968 with Foundation help, as the Young Volunteer Force

Foundation; its first director was Anthony Steen, who went on to become a Conservative MP. The Home Office review in 1973 recommended that the CDF should develop into something very similar to a national resource centre, but the process was to take twenty years. It currently describes itself as an agency whose aim is to 'help communities achieve greater control over the conditions and decisions affecting their lives'.

The Foundation's failure to persuade the government to set up a national centre for community work in 1975 marks a watershed in its Social Welfare Programme, as the idea of 'social work' was replaced by 'community development'. In 1973 the Foundation had formally withdrawn from such activities as prison aftercare, delinquency prevention and counselling, and special education. In 1974 a grant of £12,000 to help the National Council for the Unmarried Mother and her Child to reform as the National Council for One Parent Families signalled the end of the Foundation's involvement in this area.

Although the government's Voluntary Service Unit had rejected the idea of a national centre, it was more sympathetic to the idea of a national forum, and also proposed that the Foundation should, with government help, set up a pilot community resource centre in Glasgow as a test-bed for, and a precursor of, a series of local and regional centres. Responsibility for advising the Foundation on these projects fell to a committee chaired by David Jones, the then Principal of the National Institute for Social Work.

The first of the committee's three functions was to set up and monitor the Glasgow project, which became located in the high-unemployment area of Govan in the south-west of the city. Opening its doors in July 1977, Govan Area Resource Centre (GARC) was run by a management committee of local people, employing a staff of four, and provided neighbourhood organisations with a range of services, including access to reprographic facilities, to meeting space, information on wider community work resources, consultancy funding and a variety of small grants. As part of its commitment to helping communities to help themselves, the Foundation made a significant financial commitment of £61,900. European as well UK government money also underpinned the project, and a great deal of staff time and energy went into making it happen.

Significantly, GARC established an Employment Study Group, which brought together local people to address the critical issue of rising unem-

Alexander Stephen House, former headquarters of the Alexander Stephen shipyard. The building was refurbished by Govan Workspace at a cost of £1.1 million and re-opened in 1996.
Photos: Govan Workspace Ltd.

ployment. Its most lasting contribution was its research into the feasibility of establishing a managed workspace operation. As a result, Govan Workspace Ltd started life as an independent community business in 1981, its first project being the conversion of an old school into premises for small enterprises. It continues in business today, having developed two further projects, employing around 500 people. The Govan Workspace formula became a model, not just for community work, but was also quickly adopted by the public sector and eventually by private businesses.

The second part of the Jones Committee's job was to direct the monitoring and evaluation of a number of other local centres, and the third was to set up and administer the national forum on community work. By 1978, however, the third part of the remit had to be abandoned, as there was no money forthcoming to finance the forum, and there was opposition from the Association of Community Workers. However, committee meetings at the hospitable Portland Place created just the space for the exchange of ideas between people with very diverse interests in community work, in a way that neither the Community Development Foundation nor the Association of Community Workers, each with their vested positions, was able to do. Indeed, as David Thomas shrewdly argues, 'The Jones Committee was not just a forum but in its practice became, too, a surrogate national centre for community development; as such it bridged the gap between the failure of the Serota proposal for a national centre and the emergence of the Griffiths proposals in 1983 to help to transform the Community Development Foundation into a national centre.'

Community Art

In Peter Brinson's view, as he told the community artist Su Braden, artists were 'social animators or social engineers', and as he brought the different strands of the Foundation's work closer together, it was logical to set them to work on developing community art. He was convinced that 'the artist has lost his relationship to society and it's no longer absolutely clear why he's there, what he should be doing'. As someone with direct experience of trying to communicate the value of dance to a wider public through Ballet for All, his ruling idea was to close the gap that had opened up.

'Community' had become the watchword of artists inspired by the optimism of the 1960s to believe that cultural revolution was on the horizon. But the apparent failure of the 1968 protest movement to achieve radical social change, and the conservative reaction that followed, led advocates of alternative art to ask themselves whether the very structure of their art forms and the nature of their institutional support were not part of the problem, rather than the solution. One of these was Su Braden, who had experienced the dilemma at first hand when she was part of a Foundation-funded project, Pavilions in the Parks. This was an artist-led initiative to challenge the social and cultural conventions imposed by the architecture of orthodox cultural spaces. The 'pavilions' were lightweight structures set up in public parks, and used to display art 'where people naturally take their leisure'. The art shown was selected on the basis of a draw from amongst those who had offered work, thus eliminating the controlling power of a curator.

The Pavilions in the Parks project, here in Euston Square 1970, displayed art 'where people naturally take their leisure' and was presented in Chelsea, Camden, Blackheath, Cardiff and Newport. Photo: Su Braden.

The project ran from 1967 to 1971, and was seen in parks in Chelsea, Blackheath, Camden, Cardiff and Newport. But Braden for one was dissatisfied, because such schemes:

> offered no real attack on the nerve of the assumptions generally held by both 'artists' and 'non-artists' about their respective roles. They were simply under-funded alternatives to the accepted views, and as such, when judged by those who maintained both 'standards' and the purse strings, could be dismissed as 'unprofessional'.

It was out of the reappraisal of both the cultural and political relationship between artists and society that the community art movement was born.

Arguably, the Foundation had first become involved in this contentious area in 1962, when it gave a two-year grant worth £10,000 to Arnold Wesker's Centre 42. The playwright named his organisation after a Trades Union Congress resolution (no. 42) calling for more union participation in the arts, his idea being to hold popular arts festivals across the country. Seven were held in 1962, but the problems caused by the acquisition of an old engine-turning shed in Camden – although it led to the survival of the building to this day as the arts centre the Roundhouse – proved the organisation's financial nemesis, and Centre 42 folded in 1970.

The Foundation made a better investment in 1969 when it was

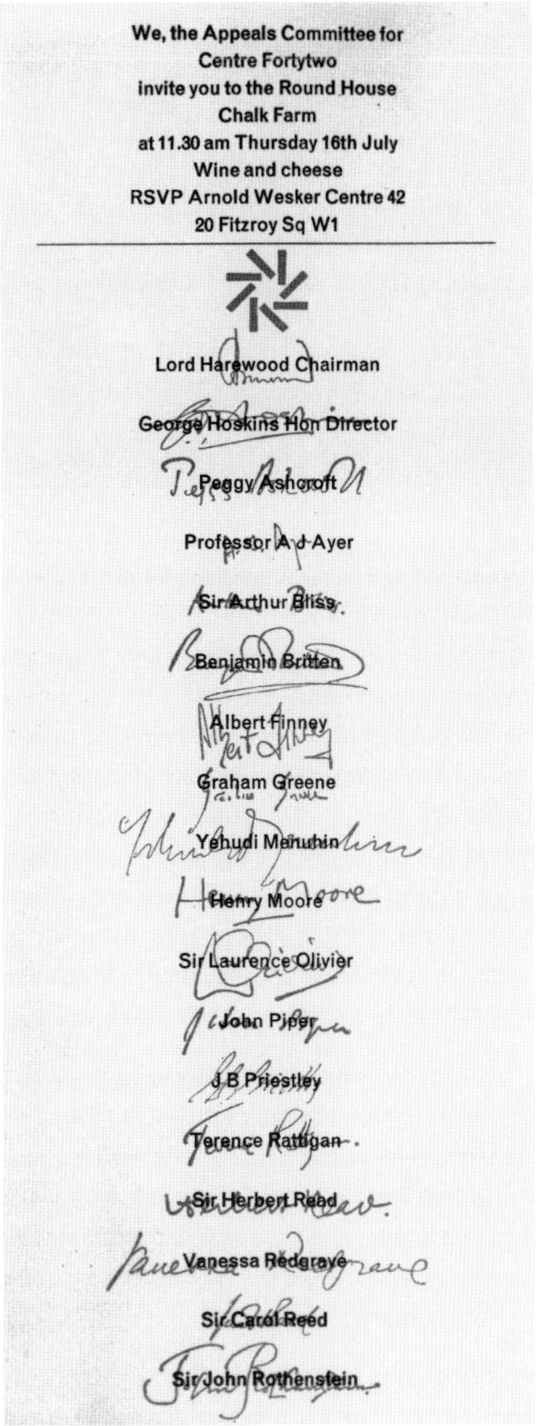

We, the Appeals Committee for
Centre Fortytwo
invite you to the Round House
Chalk Farm
at 11.30 am Thursday 16th July
Wine and cheese
RSVP Arnold Wesker Centre 42
20 Fitzroy Sq W1

Lord Harewood Chairman

George Hoskins Hon Director

Peggy Ashcroft

Professor A J Ayer

Sir Arthur Bliss

Benjamin Britten

Albert Finney

Graham Greene

Yehudi Menuhin

Henry Moore

Sir Laurence Olivier

John Piper

J B Priestley

Terence Rattigan

Sir Herbert Read

Vanessa Redgrave

Sir Carol Reed

Sir John Rothenstein

An invitation from the Appeals Committee for Centre 42, to which the Foundation gave a launching grant of £10,000 in 1962. The organisation 'aimed to reach an audience for the arts ... at present almost untouched.'

approached by a young American, a former Rhodes scholar, Ed Berman, who had been running a lunchtime theatre in Notting Hill. Berman, who has described himself as 'social entrepreneur, playwright, theatre director and producer, educationalist', exemplifies the contentious and creative spirit of the Sixties. He started in theatre, but rapidly moved on from creating new ways of making theatre to new ways of shaping society. Like other funding bodies after them, the Foundation was uncertain as to which Department should deal with Berman's application: was his project art, or was it welfare? It was decided that the Great and the Good of the Arts Committee should be consulted, but that Richard Mills, being in charge of Social Welfare, should advise them. It is an indication of the compartmentalisation of the Foundation before Brinson that Mills should remember events in these terms:

> The Arts Committee was still operating a policy based on the Bridges Report and felt disinclined to depart from it at that point. But before a decision was taken to offer support under Social Welfare, I was required to speak to the application at a meeting of the Committee. It was my first appearance before a body which hitherto appeared as exotic and remote as Marco Polo's China. It was a pleasant surprise to find them wholly sympathetic towards the project and community arts generally.

Accordingly, the Foundation awarded £15,000 over three years from the Social Welfare budget 'to help meet the cost of administration of educational and community work projects to be carried out by a group of professional writers and actors, who have come together under the title of "Inter-Action"'.

Inter-Action thrived not only as a continually evolving group of theatre companies, but as a source of community action. After surviving in squatted buildings for several years, it was able to establish its own premises in Kentish Town in 1971, assisted by what was then a sizeable grant of £25,000 from the Foundation. (These two grants would amount to more than £300,000 today.) In 1972 Inter-Action opened the first ever City Farm, and it continued to spawn new organisations such as Gay Sweatshop (1975) and the Weekend Arts College (1978). Now renamed InterChange, it has proved one of the most enduring of all the community arts projects.

Arts activities thus were already being used as a tool of community development when Brinson took over as Director. In 1970 a well-established community centre in Deptford, the Albany, run by Paul Curno (who was

Arts and Community. The exterior of Albany's Victorian building transformed by John Upton's mural, 1970. Photo: Chris Schwarz.

Centreprise, the experimental community centre/bookshop in a 'socially developing
neighbourhood in Hackney and North-East London', supported by the Foundation, 1971–3.
Photo: Centreprise.

later to join the United Kingdom Branch), was funded to employ an 'arts development worker'. In 1971 the Foundation supported the formation of Centreprise, a community resource in Hackney built around a paperback bookshop that continues to flourish. The Foundation supported it into the 1980s. During the 1970s and 1980s the Foundation gave a number of grants to assist the Craigmillar Festival Society, which became an exemplar of an arts and social project developed by the community itself.

Craigmillar is a satellite estate on the outskirts of Edinburgh, built in the late 1930s and allowed to develop appalling social problems as a result of the lack of work and the absence of facilities. An earlier grant from the Foundation had enabled Edinburgh University to study the estate and its problems, but it was when a resident, Helen Crummy, was refused violin lessons for her son by her local education authority – at a time when the Edinburgh International Festival was in full swing – that her campaign to articulate the estate's problems began. With a friend, Alice Henderson, Crummy used her local mothers' group to put on a children's show to bring residents together. This developed into an annual summer show out of

Granton Suitcase Circus, Edinburgh, 1978.
Photo: Edinburgh Film Workshop.

which the Craigmillar Festival Society was born. As Crummy has written, 'The Foundation was quick to appreciate how art had become the catalyst and helped crystallise our ideas and put them into practice by funding art, social welfare and educational projects.' In 1976 the Society went over the heads of Edinburgh's councillors to secure a £750,000 grant from the European Community that allowed them to employ professional planning, communications and arts directors. Recruited as Arts Director, the circus specialist Reg Bolton created a Community Circus School in Craigmillar's arts centre, starting a movement that spread across Scotland and beyond. In 1992 the Foundation supported the publication of Helen Crummy's story of the Craigmillar Festival Society, *Let The People Sing!*

Closing the Gap: the Fringe and Artist Placements

As we have seen, economic realism caused the Foundation gradually to withdraw from its arts building programme, but in 1969 the decision had been taken to invest in the infrastructure of a 'fifth circuit' for touring theatre: the small-scale theatres and arts centres that were part of the new and energetic 'fringe'. By 1975 twenty-one places had benefited from improvements to a total of £129,000. The changed nature of theatre is indicated by the names of companies given assistance in 1974 to buy transport and equipment: Belt and Braces Roadshow, Bubble Theatre, Brighton Combination, Crystal Theatre of the Saint, Emma Theatre Co., Footsbarn, the Half Moon Theatre, and Medium Fair Theatre Co. In 1973 the radical and adventurous Welfare State, which, like Footsbarn, Bubble and the Half Moon, continues to function, received a grant of £3,500. The Foundation had already begun to support three organisations that sought to overcome the physical and social isolation of visual artists: John Latham's Artist Placement Group, which took artists out of their studios and located them in factories and businesses (an idea later taken up by Simon Roodhouse at Yorkshire Arts and elsewhere – see Sue Hercombe's 1986 report for the Foundation, *What the hell do we want an artist here for?*); the Artists Information Registry, which became the AIR Gallery in 1975; and SPACE, set up by Bridget Riley and Peter Sedgley in 1968 to find artists low-

'The entry of the Explorers', a summer holiday show for children by Solent Song & Dance, which purchased sound equipment and musical instruments with the Foundation's help in 1975. Photo: Peter Day.

Footsbarn Theatre, which received a grant for a new van in 1974, in a scene from *Legend*, a story of Cornish tin miners and the 'little people', 1975. Photo: David Clark.

Theatre Mobile, Mid-Pennine Touring Theatre Company, purchased a new van with help from the Foundation in 1976. Photo: Northwestern Newspaper Co. Ltd.

cost studios, which continues to operate with Arts Council England funding, creating a model that has been widely adopted.

In 1972 Brinson put his policy of closing the gap between artist and community into action by launching a new programme to place professional artists in schools: £30,000 was allocated to funding three urban and four rural education authorities to employ an artist for up to two years. The difference between this and other schemes was that the artist was not expected to teach, but simply be given a place in which to work, plus the security of a salary. Among the seven were a composer, photographer, sculptor and film-maker. The details of the individual enterprises and those that followed can be found in the independent study commissioned by Brinson from Su Braden, and published with Foundation support as *Artists and People* in 1978. In Braden's view, perhaps half of these first residencies

Steeplejack Peter Tatham working on a chimney demolition in Salford. A photograph by Daniel Meadows, photographer-in-residence 1975–7 at Nelson and Colne College of Further Education, Lancashire. Courtesy of Daniel Meadows.

proved successful, and the Foundation introduced changes when it followed up in 1975 with six two-year residencies, re-titled 'Artists-in-the-Community'. The second scheme was designed to ensure a better partnership by ensuring that the community in question genuinely wanted an artist in their midst, and that the scheme be jointly funded with the Arts Council or a regional arts association, local authorities having proved reluctant to fund artists in schools.

Making Community Art Work

Although the participation and support of the Foundation was vital to the development of community art, the Gulbenkian was operating alongside larger and now wealthier state-funded organisations. Community art, where the personal was the political, and the political was the cultural, presented funding bodies with a considerable challenge. There was no established genre or practice that could be pigeon-holed as community art, and no agreement even among community artists as to what its ultimate purpose was – except that the movement knew what it was against. According to Owen Kelly, a community artist active in South London funded by the Gulbenkian to produce the study *Community, Art and the State: Storming the citadels* in 1984, the lack of a theoretical definition was exploited by community artists themselves, whose instinct was to 'take the money and run'. But, Kelly argues, funding can be addictive, and in time will shape the work it funds. While the Arts Council tried to come to terms with the fractious world of community art through a series of committees and reports, the artists – like their colleagues in social work – themselves found it necessary to become better organised, risking the very institutionalisation they wanted to resist.

Both sides reached an accommodation as a result of the report of an Arts Council working party chaired by Professor Harold Baldry in 1974. The Association of Community Artists, given a start-up grant by the Gulbenkian, was able to demonstrate to the working party that there was a substantial number of people active in this new field, and Baldry duly recommended that the Arts Council should set up a community arts sub-committee that would support such work. His report gave no hostages to fortune by actually defining what community artists did, or acknowledging the political dimension to their activities. But this vagueness left the applicants exposed to the whims of their funders, first in the Arts Council, and then, when the scheme began to be devolved in 1978, in the Regional Arts Associations.

Although the sums were small in comparison to what was being given to more orthodox arts organisations, the Arts Council committed £176,000 to fifty-seven projects in 1975–6 and £300,000 to seventy-five in 1976–7, but then scaled back as a squeeze on its own funding from the government began to bite, transferring responsibility to the Regional Arts Associations. The price, moreover, was to have community art reformulated as either 'missionary' work, intended to introduce the conventional arts to those who had not experienced them before, or as ameliorative help for 'the disadvantaged'. Community art became an aspect of social provision rather than cultural revolution. The Association of Community Artists was regarded with suspicion as a 'political' organisation, and after the Arts Council refused it a grant on those grounds in 1978 it dissolved itself as a national organisation, passing on its education and information responsibilities to the Shelton Trust, formed in 1980.

The conceptual and ideological difficulties attending community art were less problematic for Peter Brinson at the Gulbenkian, who described it in the 1978 *Annual Report* as 'one of the most influential developments in the arts since the war'. But as a partner organisation whose funds were intended to initiate ideas for others to follow through, the Foundation was bound to be affected by the economic and political climate. As Brinson had warned in 1976, 'During 1975 . . . the Foundation became very conscious that it may even have to supplement the revenue assistance given to community art by public bodies if many of the most worthwhile achievements of the immediate past are not to fail'. In 1976 at least a quarter of the forty-nine projects funded by the Social Welfare Department were for community art, in 1977 the Arts, Education and Welfare Departments jointly contributed £110,320 as the Foundation's activities worked together.

Much art is ephemeral, and community art by its nature is as concerned with process as it is with product. Between 1976 and 1978 the muralist Brian Barnes, a Gulbenkian artist-in-the-community attached to the

Battersea Arts Centre in London, led a team of sixty local people in painting a mural along Battersea Bridge Road, called *The Good, the Bad, and the Ugly*. Completed in February 1978, it was demolished by developers in June 1979. Other Foundation-backed projects have proved more durable: the Paddington Print Workshop, set up with Foundation support as a community resource that would create posters and other materials to publicise local campaigns, continues as the London Print Studio, still supplying a community service with Arts Council support. Not far away are Meanwhile Gardens, a community park between the Grand Union Canal and the inner-city motorway, whose very name embodies its originally temporary nature when a young sculptor, Jamie McCullough, set about transforming it from a strip of wasteland in 1976.

The Foundation's help with salaries in 1977 and 1978 was only a part of the effort that went into Meanwhile Gardens, but the Foundation also published a short book by McCullough that is both a record of the project

A section of *The Good, the Bad and the Ugly*, a huge mural on Battersea Bridge Road created by Brian Barnes, a beneficiary of the Foundation's Artists-in-the-Community scheme, and painted over a period of two years by sixty local residents. The mural was 'unveiled' by Sir Hugh Casson in 1978 and declared 'one of the most outstanding examples of community art created in Britain today' by art critic Richard Cork in the *Evening Standard*. Photo: Brian Barnes.

Paddington Printshop, Marylands Community Centre, received a grant for the purchase of printing equipment in 1975.

The Skateboard Track at Meanwhile Gardens, 1978, a scheme which transformed 'a derelict site in a West London deprived area into a community recreational and cultural amenity for people of all ages'. Photo: Clive B. Harrison.

and a 'how to' guide for others. McCullough, who by the end of the scheme had stopped calling himself a sculptor, comments wisely: 'The building of a park would not of itself make social change; it would merely set the scene for it to happen. In a way, it was failure: but only the failure of fantasy. Reality was showing what could be done.' A similar insight into the complexities of community work – its pleasures and its pains – can be found in another Gulbenkian book, Bob Hescott's *The Feast of Fools: The story of community theatre in Nottingham*. Between 1975 and 1979 Hescott's organisation, Sociable Theatre, received £18,900 in grants from the Gulbenkian. An actor at Nottingham Playhouse, in 1973 Hescott had become involved in the theatre's Saturday children's club, and teamed up with a small group of school drama teachers and student teachers to do shows in adventure playgrounds, children's hospitals and old people's homes as well as pubs and for the annual Nottingham Festival. Some were sheer entertainment, some served as social work funded by the Commission for Racial Equality, and some took the form of agitprop against Nottingham Council.

Hescott's energy and enthusiasm shines through his account, but it is impossible not to feel that by the time his book was published in 1983 he had been worn down by bureaucratic obstacles and delays as community art was taken up by official agencies who saw it as a means of addressing rising unemployment and social distress. In 1978 Su Braden had pointed out in her book for the Gulbenkian:

> If you change the context of artistic production, then you must change the vocabulary. The truth is that the language of the international art market is mute in the context of a housing estate. What has surprised me is that this ineluctable fact seems to have escaped so many sponsors and participants of the schemes I have seen. Those artists who *have* grappled with the kernel of the problem, however, have gone some way along the path from a liberal idea to 'extend cultural awareness' to a truly revolutionary movement in the arts.

The Manpower Services Commission, however, set up in 1975, seized on community art as a capital-light but labour-intensive means of soaking up unemployment through its STEP (Special Temporary Employment Programme) and YOP (Youth Opportunity Programme) schemes that created plenty of work for community artists, but massively distorted their intentions. As Hescott describes it:

Artificial groups, not tied by any umbilical cord to the community, did way-out things with bizarre make-up and alienated the arts still further from the communities they were supposed to be serving, because they never felt the need to explain their work, their work never offered explanatory models. It clung to all the mystification of the traditional theatre, and when the money dried up, so did they.

By the time Brinson left the Gulbenkian in October 1982 the Foundation was entering a new phase in its support for community art, which gradually ceased to be funded through Social Welfare and became part of the Community Communications programme of the Education Department. While still doing what it could to fill the gaps in official funding – in 1979 £50,000 was set aside to support activities in community buildings – the Foundation responded to what was in effect the professional-isation of community art by turning to the issue of training. In 1982 it commissioned a national enquiry from Dartington Hall, out of which came the Community Arts Apprenticeship Scheme set up in association with the Regional Arts Associations and the Arts Council's training department, which ran from 1983 to 1988, and was the subject of a Foundation report, *Wanted! Community Artists*, published in 1988 and offering a model for other agencies. On leaving the Foundation, Brinson became Head of the Department for Research and Community Development at the Laban Centre for Movement and Dance at Goldsmiths College, where community art became part of the curriculum.

Ten years later, in 1992, Brinson had an opportunity to weigh the fruits of the community arts movement that he had done so much to support, by chairing a Foundation-sponsored national enquiry for the Community Development Foundation. Echoing Brinson's earlier position (see page 93), the report was still looking 'to end the artificial separation of "people" from "artists"'. Though community art was marginalised in official statistics and received relatively little subsidy, 'many millions' of people were now involved in the activity and its influence was growing. There was:

a broad acceptance within local government, health and other services that the arts have become a necessary part of public provision. By 1990, local authorities had become the most financially influential supporters and participants in the arts. Collectively they give more now to the arts than central government gives through the Arts Councils.

This shows the distance local authorities had travelled since the Bridges Report. Yet, as Brinson and his colleagues recognised, it was to be the high point of local authority patronage, as the effects of the change from the rating system to the Poll Tax and the introduction of rate-capping began to bite. 'Although the principle of arts in the community has been won to a great extent in local authorities and regional bodies, provision at this level remains patchy and unco-ordinated. The battle has yet to be won in national policy-making.'

There is also a suggestion, in Brinson's introduction to the report, that another battle had been lost. While 'outreach projects into communities' were no longer a specialist field for artists, and it was true that museums, galleries, theatre companies and so forth regularly undertook work in association with the health authorities and social services, Brinson explained that: 'The arts scene had changed. Therefore an inquiry into community arts (our original title) was inappropriate. It had to be arts in the community.' In this subtle switch of emphasis, Brinson implies, the cultural revolutionaries of the 1960s had lost out to the cultural bureaucrats of the 1990s.

The Communities Britain Ignores

Within the general debate about how to promote community development, and encourage communities to help themselves, there was one theme that was politely referred to as 'community relations', but more directly understood as 'race'. The Foundation's concern with issues of race relations began early in its history. In the summer of 1958, race riots in Nottingham and Notting Hill had attracted considerable press coverage, but issues of racism and immigration were virtually ignored in the elections of 1959 and indeed in mainstream politics, right up until Enoch Powell's infamous 'rivers of blood' speech in Birmingham in April 1968. In 1964, Richard Mills's concern about the difficulties that black people were experiencing in British society led him to suggest, in an internal policy paper, that 'the black/white

American activist Angela Davis speaking at Keskidee, the multiracial community and arts centre in North London, which received £10,100 towards salaries and lighting equipment in 1975.
Photo: Keskidee Trust.

question in this country assumes the dimensions of a major problem, and one of compelling urgency'. A large grant of £50,000 was made in 1967 to the National Committee for Commonwealth Immigrants, but his suggestion that race should become a major new area of interest for the Foundation was not fully taken up until nearly ten years later, with the arrival of Peter Brinson, when in 1973 it was decided to 'concentrate primarily on community work and race relations during the next phase'.

By this time the expulsion of 30,000 Asians from Uganda had added to the growing tension over race in Britain. The press fuelled hostility and fear with scaremongering reports such as that in a leader column in the *Daily Express* on 12 February 1971: 'There are 200,000 Asians in East Africa all possessing British passports and they will come here soon.' The following month the theme was continued in *The Daily Telegraph*: 'Kenyan Asian numbers double – 100,000 may enter Britain by the end of the year.' Throughout the decade, immigrants were portrayed as a drain on the welfare state: 'A Kenyan Asian has been given a council house ahead of 17,000 people on the local housing list within a week of arriving,' claimed the *Daily Mail* on 5 April 1976.

In accordance with its regular practice, the Foundation wanted to find ways to shed light on the issues, in order to know how to proceed. In 1974 Sir Laurence Lindo (the Jamaican High Commissioner and an Oxford running Blue) chaired a race relations forum, sponsored by the Foundation in partnership with the Community Relations Commission and the United Nations Division of Social Affairs in Geneva. Its remit was to 'elucidate policy and objectives, evaluate possible strategies for change, cost the policies proposed, and prepare a report'. The Foundation found, however, that improving community relations was a highly sensitive area, charged with anger and fraught with rivalries between the oppressed communities themselves. The government-funded Community Relations Commission turned out to lack credibility among the constituency that it was meant to benefit and it was discovered that before establishing a broader dialogue, the very different communities wanted a chance to meet amongst themselves. The Lindo forum was suspended and instead in January 1975 the Foundation supported a major conference: 'Black People in Britain – the Way Forward'.

This was the first time that representatives of West Indian and Asian interest groups had come together in a politically meaningful way to try to fight racism. The conference resulted in the formation of a committee to 'take steps towards the creation of a permanent national black people's organisation to represent both Asian and Afro/West Indians, to work for more effective anti-discriminatory legislation and other measures to secure parity of treatment irrespective of colour, race or religion.' With Foundation support the committee consulted widely with over 700 organisations, and a follow-up conference was held in Birmingham in July 1976. This turned out to be a fractious occasion, with determined disruption by a minority among

Peter Brinson,
Director of the
Foundation's UK
Branch, speaks at the
1975 conference
'Black People in
Britain – the Way
Forward'.
Photo: Syd Burke.

the 400 delegates. In spite of this, a majority approved the adoption of the key points of the proposed constitution for a National Organisation of African, Asian and Caribbean People. This held its first annual general meeting the following year, but although it had Foundation backing, the organisation did not get off the ground, when such agreement as had been achieved at Birmingham broke down.

Richard Mills later described this disappointment as only 'an apparent failure'; in fact the conferences and the energy generated by the Foundation's engagement helped move the debate, and practice, on. As far as the Foundation was concerned, the way forward was to start to fund directly individual black self-help groups such as day-care centres and community centres – for instance a Bangla education and cultural centre, and Bristol Caribbean Community Enterprises – while continuing to help organisations such as the Runnymede Trust, founded in 1968 'to promote a successful multi-ethnic Britain', which in 1974 was given a grant of £15,000 over three years to cover basic running costs.

The press were again heightening racial tension in 1976, reporting on 6 May: 'Invasion of Asians forces Borough to call for Help' (*The Daily Telegraph*); 'Another 20,000 Asians are on the Way (*The Sun*); 'New Flood of

Soul Kids – Adoption Resource Exchange campaigns for 'real family life', 1975.
Photo: Armet Francis.

Moonshine
Community Arts
Workshop's summer
festival in Brent,
1977.
Photo: MCAW.

'The Festival of Languages brings together those who normally speak another language
at home and those who learn their languages in the classroom', Birmingham, 1988.
Photo: Ray Peters.

Asians to Britain' (*Mirror*). It was against this background that Naseem Khan researched and wrote her seminal report *The Arts Britain Ignores*, funded by the Gulbenkian in conjunction with the Arts Council and the Community Relations Commission. Naseem Khan had co-edited one of the earliest black community newspapers in the 1970s, *The Hustler*, and went on to found the Minorities Arts Advisory Service (MAAS), the national umbrella body for black and Asian arts. Following the Gulbenkian's usual practice, Khan's report was supported by a committee whose terms of reference were to describe:

> the contributions which Afro-Caribbean-Asian communities and arts activities are making to British Society . . . to review the economic aspect . . . to assess what latent artistic talents can be encouraged by an increase in resources . . . and to consider how to improve culturally the lives of minority and majority populations through increased accessibility to these arts activities.

The report concluded, as its title suggests, that the arts establishment was failing to respond to, or to nurture, the growth of ethnic minority arts, and recommended increased awareness and increased funding. In doing so it started a debate that continues to this day about the extent to which minority arts are helped (in that they get specific funding streams) or hindered (in that they are categorised as separate from other arts) by being given special attention. But the report did help to shift attitudes, so that less than ten years later the Foundation was able to note that 'whereas ethnic diversity was once seen principally as the cause of problems to be remedied, now more often, especially in the arts, it is proposed as a fit subject for celebration.' The Foundation became an important funder of black and Asian arts companies.

Closing the Gap: Helping the Artist

Community art was not Brinson's sole preoccupation. The month he arrived at Portland Place the Foundation published *Training in the Conservation of Paintings*, the conclusions of a two-year enquiry in partnership with the Museum and Galleries Commission. Its main proposal was that the government should establish a national institution for the training of conservators, and the Foundation set aside £150,000 towards the cost. The government did not rise to the bait, however, and it was not until 1976 that the Gulbenkian was able, with a consortium of other private trusts, to fund the establishment of the Hamilton Kerr Institute as a department of the Fitzwilliam Museum in Cambridge. Support was also given for a conservators' course at the Courtauld Institute.

Vocational training became an important theme in Brinson's time and beyond: in two reports commissioned by the Foundation, Lord Vaizey addressed drama education in *Going on the Stage* (1975) and music in *Training Musicians* (1978), and Brinson supported dance, as we shall see. The Foundation continued to emphasise the importance of the individual artist, through residencies, commissions, bursaries or purchases. By the time the Music Commissioning Fund was merged with the Dance Fund in 1975, forty-six awards had been made since 1960. The same year the music fellowship scheme that had run from 1967 to 1971 was revived, and ran till 1979, awarding a total of thirty-eight fellowships since it began. Between 1973 and 1976 the Foundation ran an awards scheme for film-makers in partnership with the Regional Arts Associations, and between 1976 and 1978 ten two-year bursaries were given to visual artists.

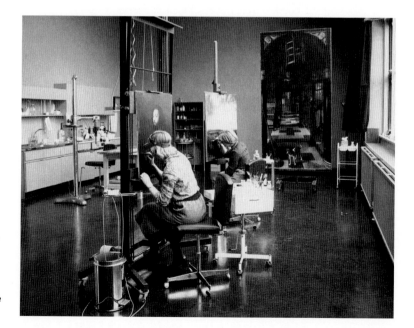

Training in the conservation and restoration of paintings at the Hamilton Kerr Institute, Cambridge. The Foundation pledged £150,000 for a conservation institute in 1972. Photo: Alex Starkey. © Country Life Picture Library.

Scottish Opera's Opera for Youth touring unit, which received a grant of £10,000 in
1975. Workshop for *The Mountain People* by Peter Naylor and Cliff Hanby.
Photo: Eric Thorburn.

Roger Lambert watching the shooting of his film *I Want to be Famous* – one of a number of young film-makers to receive an award under the Foundation's Programme of Assistance to Film, 1973–6.

Welcome as these different schemes were to their beneficiaries, the Foundation found the process of selection and administration very time-consuming. In October 1979 a private report, *Help to Artists*, was sent to the Trustees in Lisbon that argued:

> Support for the creation of individual works, on commission or assisted by grants, contributes less to the artist's eventual long-term success ... The conclusion must be that the Foundation's awards are most useful when they provide the opportunity for the artist to develop over a number of years, either on one grant or a series of linked grants.

The eighteen awards made to film-makers, for instance, 'had only an ephemeral impact on the artists' careers. Successful films resulted, but the awards did nothing to resolve underlying financial and production problems facing the film-makers.'

Creative artists remained a long-standing commitment, but in 1979 the Foundation announced a shift of emphasis, following the establishment of an Access to the Arts Committee in 1978, itself the result of a 1977 conference on adult education and the arts. Anticipating by twenty years the arguments of New Labour, the Foundation wished to see greater access to the arts in general, while, as it said in the 1979 *Annual Report*, it felt that individual artists were now being better catered for than previously by the Arts Council and the Regional Arts Associations. 'Problems seem to exist however for artists who wish to explore and test ideas in media where practice is expensive ... Future assistance will be designed to help the artist gain access to appropriate resources, thus furthering his or her development.' Rather than ensuring an artist's mere survival, the Foundation would turn increasingly to supporting innovation and experiment.

Education

In 1976 the Foundation staff became concerned about the education and training of the 16–19 age group, and about what they saw as neglected minorities in education. The first step was to get these issues accepted as Foundation priorities for consultation. Once this was done, two working groups were set up and each of them then had a series of meetings and contacts with interested parties such as government departments, local authorities, trades unions and academics. They also consulted people in the target groups themselves.

Each working group then produced a written report that was circulated for comment, and after revision, the papers' recommendations were put forward as priorities for grant-giving. This whole process took about a year. However, it did not stop there. The Foundation realised that its own limited resources could only go so far in addressing the problems, but found that through its investigatory and consultative processes it had created a body of evidence and a constituency of concern that extended beyond its own interests in effective grant-giving. In fact the Foundation concluded, as it said in 1978, that perhaps

> the best contribution to a social problem as large as inner-city education was to 'rouse and inform', that is rouse public concern through well-based information which helps clarify the situation and indicates solutions. In this way limited resources can make a considerable impact.

Brinson's final report for the Foundation was *The Arts in Schools*, published in 1982, and researched and edited by the educationist Ken Robinson. This highly influential report laid down a marker for the involvement of artists in schools, with particularly persuasive chapters on how the arts add richness and depth to young people's lives. At a time when the role of the arts in a potential national curriculum was being debated, the report was well received by schools and helped consolidate the place of the arts in school life, although bizarrely while music and visual arts became curriculum subjects, drama was subsumed within English, and dance became part of physical education. The report served as a counterweight to the politicians' enthusiasm for education to focus on science and technology. The Foundation encouraged the Arts Council to address the issue of arts and education by funding the first post for an arts education officer.

The Arts in Schools was the beginning of a long campaign, supported by the Foundation to keep the arts at the heart of school life. Without it there would have been no National Advisory Committee on Creative and Cultural Education, established in 1998. This committee, chaired by the same Ken Robinson, produced the report *All Our Futures,* published in 1999. It argued that young people in the twenty-first century would need to develop a new set of skills, attitudes and competencies in order to cope with the growing complexity and diversity of economic and social life. In practice, the demands of the main National Curriculum subjects were squeezing the arts out of school life, provoking fears that concentration on the content of learning would stifle creativity.

Although *All Our Futures* showed that the argument in favour of the arts in schools was far from won, it provoked a significant response from the politicians. The decision was taken to establish a new scheme, Creative Partnerships, backed with £30 million of government funding. The scheme relies heavily on professional expertise developed through the support of the Foundation for artists working in schools over the last thirty years. In 2001, Chris Smith, New Labour's Secretary of State for Culture, said, 'I want to see us put creativity at the heart of education, encouraging our children to develop their talents', while the Education Secretary Charles Clarke conceded in a speech in June 2003: 'Creativity isn't an add-on. It must form a vital and integral part of every child's experience of school.' It was a case that the Foundation had been arguing for years.

'Untrod Territory': Dance

When it came to combining arts education and the practice of art itself, not surprisingly, in view of Peter Brinson's tastes and experience, the Foundation was most conspicuously successful in the field of dance. The policy of supporting modern dance had got under way during Dunbar's directorship, with substantial awards to Ballet Rambert, and to Northern Dance and London Contemporary Dance, both given launch grants by the Foundation in 1969. In future years the Foundation played a significant role in helping the American-born choreographer Robert Cohan to establish the Contemporary Dance Trust both as a company, London Contemporary Dance Theatre, and as a school, the London School of Contemporary Dance, stepping in with £30,000 to rescue the company at a critical moment. As a teacher and choreographer Cohan was able to nurture an entire generation of dance artists and turn a minority interest into an increasingly popular art form.

London Contemporary Dance Theatre in *Nympheas* by Robert Cohan. The Foundation provided funding in 1974 for the School to develop its choreographic department. Photo: Anthony Crickmay. © Theatre Museum.

In 1971 two parallel schemes were set up, a Dance Commissioning Fund to help companies employ choreographers and designers to make new work and a Dance Awards Fund to help broaden the experience of composers, designers and choreographers. Both ran until 1975, when the Music and Dance Commissioning Funds were amalgamated. The Foundation found that, because of the Arts Council's relative neglect of dance, 'it could explore almost untrod territory'. Accordingly, that year a further £90,000 was earmarked for 'the first large-scale dance programme prepared by any foundation in Britain'. Between 1956 and 1975 the Foundation invested £285,838 in dance, of which £214,960 was committed after 1971.

In March 1974 the Foundation organised an 'action conference' on dance education that brought together experts from right across the field and led to the publication in 1980 of a key Gulbenkian study, *Dance Education and Training in Britain*. The Arts and the Education Departments worked together to develop a system of dance education to give assistance to a would-be dancer from the age of 14 until becoming a professional, and at the same time helped companies refresh their repertoires with new works. In 1975 the Foundation organised its first two-week residential summer school for choreographers and composers, which in 1976 became a

Extemporary Dance Group received funds under the Dance Commissioning Scheme in
1975 for three short works. Corrine Bougaard in Micha Bergese's piece *Worksongs*.
Photo: Clive Boursnell.

fixture at the University of Surrey, the first step towards the establishment of Britain's first chair in dance studies and the creation of the present dance studies department at the University. Eight choreographers and eight composers worked together with musicians and dancers under the direction of a celebrated choreographer – Glen Tetley, Norman Morrice and Robert Cohan successively.

Robert Cohan taking a class at the Foundation's National Choreographic Summer School in 1978. Photo: Anthony Crickmay. © V&A Images/Theatre Museum.

In a classic example of the Foundation's ability to launch a project and then hand it on to others, in 1979, with money from the European Union and the British, Canadian and Australian Arts Councils, the summer school became the International Dance Course for Professional Choreographers and Composers. The early days are described in Annette Massie's 1983 Foundation report, *Dance in Time*. Having succeeded with dance, in 1979 the Foundation launched the New Theatre Workshop, a similar summer school for playwrights, with directors and actors on hand, which ran until 1982, and is described in Christie Dickason's study, *Experience and Experiment*. In 1979 the Foundation made a first grant of £7,000 to Dance Umbrella, founded by Val Bourne as a management service to small dance companies, and best known for its annual festival, which was responsible for the explosion of interest in contemporary dance in the 1980s.

Dance Umbrella's conference on 'Dance in Education', 1979. Photo: Dance Umbrella.

The Redcliffe-Maud Report

Back in 1974 Brinson had expressed the Foundation's 'regret at the fractured nature of official support for the arts in Britain, particularly between what is looked upon as fine arts, and what is looked upon as arts-and-education, much of which is under-subsidised'. He was then in the process of setting up a new enquiry into the structure of arts funding in Britain, intended to do for the 1970s what the Bridges Report had done for the 1960s.

The enquiry was conducted by Lord Redcliffe-Maud, who had chaired the Royal Commission on Local Government prior to the Local Government Act of 1972. His report, published in 1976 as *Support for the Arts in England and Wales,* is best remembered for defining the 'arm's-length principle', the convention by which politicians were kept at arm's length from the decisions about the money they allocated to the arts.

> By self-denying ordinance the politicians leave the [Arts] Council free to spend as it thinks fit. No Minister needs to reply to questions in Parliament about the beneficiaries – or about unsuccessful applicants for an Arts Council grant. A convention has been established over the years that in arts patronage neither the politician nor the bureaucrat knows best.

Redcliffe-Maud's benign view reflects the consensual spirit of the post-war years when politicians, bureaucrats and most artists were sufficiently like-minded for state patronage not to require overt direction. But that situation was about to change, for 'inflation, unemployment and our debts to foreigners compel us to take stock'. Where the Bridges Report examined the internal needs of the sector, Redcliffe-Maud had to address an external crisis: 'At the time of writing the arts are in such dire financial straits that all we can do is to secure survival.'

Whereas the Bridges Report found Britain's arts funding system to be 'rather scrappy and patchy' (see pages 46–9), it was now 'highly complex and confusing'. Redcliffe-Maud could hardly avoid stating the obvious: 'What artists and the arts in Britain most of all need is money.' While £5,000 million a year was being spent on education, less than £100 million was going on all forms of art, including museums and galleries. 'It would be one of the most important developments of the next decade in Britain if the arts became central and not peripheral to our education system.' As we have seen, this was not the direction education policy was to take, in spite of the efforts of the Gulbenkian.

Consistent with the view of the Bridges Report, Redcliffe-Maud's solution to the funding crisis was more local democracy, where he hoped, forlornly as it turned out, that local government, when given a statutory duty to foster the arts, would become 'the chief art patrons of the long-term future'. While supporting the existence of the Arts Council, Redcliffe-Maud wanted to see more power devolved locally. He called for the creation of separate Councils for Wales and Scotland and a new concordat with the Regional Art Associations, which should not become 'regional outposts' of central bodies. Here, as we saw in chapter two, Redcliffe-Maud's recommendations had more success. The Arts Council was sympathetic to devolution and, following the government-ordered Wilding Report of 1989, it became official policy, only to be reversed in 2001 with the abolition of the Regional Arts Boards. Scotland and Wales acquired independent Councils in 1994. Redcliffe-Maud's call for a Minister of Cabinet rank finally became a reality in 1992 with the creation of the Department of National Heritage, but, contrary to Redcliffe-Maud's suggestion, the arts have remained separate from education.

Although Redcliffe-Maud's ideas extended well beyond the Foundation's purse, over time a number of his ideas have achieved reality. He called for a much more positive attitude towards helping the disabled participate in the arts. Although his suggestion that the arts be zero-rated for Value Added Tax was ignored, he gave useful support for the institution of a Public Lending Right to compensate authors for the use of their work in public libraries. He foresaw the Tate Gallery developing regional outposts. He wanted to see the Museums and Galleries Commission become a more pro-active body, a call partially answered by the formation of the Museums, Libraries and Archives Council in 2000, and wanted to see a strengthened Crafts Council and British Film Institute. And in one area he found that the Gulbenkian could be of immediate help. He concluded his main recommendations with the comment that 'Now is the time, despite financial problems, to make our arts available to other countries and their arts to us.' In 1976, backed by a commitment of £45,000 from the Foundation, the Arts Council and the British Council came together to set up the Visiting Arts Unit, which continues to act as a key agency for foreign arts companies coming to this country.

Cities

The Foundation's concern for life in the inner city reflects a certain natural order, in that its attention focuses where problems exist. From the earliest days, as we have seen, social welfare projects were funded in London, Birmingham, Liverpool and other cities. In 1973 inner-city education was adopted as a priority for the Education Programme, and two action conferences were organised by the Labour MP Frank Field. The composition of the committees reflects a broad political spectrum, including as it did both Dr Rhodes Boyson, then a headmaster, but who was to become an outspoken Minister for Education under Margaret Thatcher, and the left-leaning philosopher Professor Stuart Hampshire.

Charities and government were troubled by the state of the inner cities and they were not alone. While the flight from cities in the 1970s was most starkly illustrated by the well-publicised near anarchy of New York, closer to home crumbling buildings, industrial decline, mounting poverty and rising crime in British cities caused widespread public concern. Billed as a Gulbenkian/*Sunday Times* event, the 'Save Our Cities' conference on inner-city problems was held in Bristol in February 1977, and the writer and journalist Rosemary Righter's booklet of the same name was published immediately afterwards.

Not explicitly connected, but almost undoubtedly influenced by the conference, in June 1977 the Labour Government's White Paper on inner cities called for the full involvement of local communities, voluntary agencies and industry in regeneration. Another result of 'Save Our Cities' was the appointment of Paul Curno in February 1978 on a 'three-year contract to implement the proposals of the David Jones Committee and to work with the voluntary and community sectors in the inner-city areas of the thirteen cities the government had selected for special attention and additional funding.'

Like Peter Brinson, he was well known to the Foundation, having been a recipient of grants while Director of the Albany. His career path was unusual, even for a Gulbenkian employee. Curno had been a Franciscan friar but later owned a bistro in Kensington called *La Bonne Bouche*. He had experience both as a House Father in a remand centre and as a social work adviser, and he was heavily concerned with Settlements, both professionally and in a

Arthur Scargill,
President of the
National Union of
Mineworkers, speaks
in Trafalgar Square at
the People's March for
Jobs, Liverpool –
London, 1981.
Photo: Halewood
Unemployed Group.

voluntary capacity. Before joining the Foundation, while Chairman of the Blackfriars Settlement, he had been involved in the Coin Street campaign.

The focus on partnerships and community solutions that came out of 'Save Our Cities' was explored further in 1978 when the Gulbenkian was involved in planning a conference, jointly with the National Council of Social Service and the supermarket chain Tesco, called 'Partners in the City'. The focus was on how non-statutory groups might best work with the government on inner-city issues.

The next major cities initiative came in 1980 with the decision to organise another conference, 'Community Challenge', this time sponsored jointly with *The Guardian* and held in Liverpool in September 1981. It was given added urgency by the very recent riots in the city's Toxteth area. The conference organiser was Charles Clarke, who in 2004 became Home Secretary. The event proved problematic. The organising idea was to bring together local authorities, businesses, trades unions and voluntary groups from fifteen cities so that they might learn from each other's experiences. It was felt that a venue outside London would show commitment to the regions. But the Gulbenkian's good intentions were undermined by a cabal of about thirty hard Leftists, who questioned the right of the Foundation, as an unelected body, to organise the conference, and who proceeded to pass a series of motions directing how the Gulbenkian should in future spend its money.

Community Communications: Finding a Voice

One conclusion of 'Save Our Cities' in 1977 was a recognition that inner-city voices were unheard and that they needed to find a means of expression. 'The development of community communications was the way to do it.' This realisation coincided with the 1977 White Paper *Report of the Committee on the Future of Broadcasting* by that friend of the Foundation, Lord Annan. The report's 174 recommendations transformed the practice and regulation of broadcasting, in particular opening up new opportunities in local radio. The Foundation entered into collaboration with the BBC, the Independent Broadcasting Authority and the Manpower Services Commission to produce the 1979 Gulbenkian report *Broadcasting and Youth*.

The report had been sparked by concern about the plight of the post-school generation in industrialised societies, emerging from education into a world of unemployment. It suggested that broadcasting could do more, both to entertain and educate this group, and pondered how broadcasters might expand and improve their co-operation with other agencies and directly with young people. A youthful Peter Mandelson, then Chairman of the British Youth Council and now a European Commissioner, headed a follow-up investigation into how the report's recommendations might be put into practice, principally by finding ways for young people and broadcasters to enter into dialogue by means of a Young Adult Unit. The Advisory Committee for this feasibility study was chaired by Sara Morrison, also Chair of the NCVO and a member of the Annan Committee.

In 1978 'Community Communications' was taken up as one of four new priorities adopted 'after the most thorough reappraisal of the Branch's work for five years' (others were inner cities, community self-help and the think-tank/publication emphasis). To a degree this policy statement reflected a

Photograph from *Come to Kingsland Market*, written and illustrated by children from a Southampton school with the help of photographer-in-residence, 1980. Photo: Corinne Davidson.

Shankill Photo Workshop. *The Shankill Bulletin* received a grant in 1984 to encourage educational, arts and cultural activities in Belfast.

practice that had been in place for some time. At the level of individual grant-giving, community communications had been supported from the mid-1970s through a wide variety of initiatives such as Radio Doom, which worked with handicapped and deprived children, Liberation Films, the Avon Community Communications Association and the Adamstown Community Centre's Photographic exhibition. Inter-Action had been funded to run video workshops. However, as a result of the policy shift Joan Munro was appointed in 1980 on a two-year contract as Development Officer for this strand of work, 'to explore how community workers could use video, tape/slide, exhibitions and other means to promote community action'.

The idea of communities finding a voice affected all three of the Foundation's Programmes as a philosophical touchstone as much as a series of initiatives built around communication. The Foundation went out to look for those without a voice. An example of this is the Warnock Committee that reported in 1978. Under the leadership of Mary Warnock, the moral philosopher and author who was to become a life peer and Mistress of Girton College, Cambridge, this committee looked at 'a range of need which was different from the needs of the 16–19 age group on the one hand and from the well-recognised needs of the ethnic minorities', namely the education, care and employment of handicapped young people. Simultaneously, the Foundation was looking for other 'voiceless' groups: travellers, gypsies, the homeless, children in hospitals and in care, the mentally, physically and emotionally handicapped, and old people.

1979: a Change of Government

Peter Brinson's directorship had begun with external and internal change. Even greater changes took place as it drew to a close. The Conservative election victory of 1979 brought to power a government determined to reverse the country's perceived economic and social decline by breaking up the post-war consensus that had sought to keep in balance the interests of central government, the local authorities, business, the trades unions, the voluntary sector and the semi-corporate public services that sustained education, health, broadcasting, the arts and other institutions of the welfare state. Determined to reduce government expenditure (but to increase central government control) Mrs Thatcher and her ministers set out to replace the values of collectivism with those of individual enterprise. The market would be the new model for society; failure in the market was no one's responsibility but one's own. If increased unemployment was necessary to drive down inflation – which in 1980 was running at 20.9 per cent – then unemployment – which rose to over 3 million by 1982 – was a price worth paying.

This cultural counter-revolution had an immediate effect on all aspects of the Foundation's work as the government cut back its financial commitment to the arts, education and welfare, while at the same time seeking to restructure the institutions that provided them in order to exchange a 'dependency culture' for an 'enterprise culture'. The Arts Council sustained an immediate mid-year cut of £1 million, and responded by ceasing to fund forty-one companies. Local authority arts budgets fell by as much as 70 per cent. It must have been especially depressing to Peter Brinson that between 1980 and 1982, one quarter of the main small-scale dance companies closed. As he reported in 1980:

> New arts activities are now inhibited everywhere and many established arts
> organisations are extremely worried about their futures . . . many organisations
> and artists have already sought help from the Foundation in replacing public
> subsidy, but the Foundation's resources do not allow it to respond to these
> requests.

The retreat of the state from its responsibility to nurture developments, not only in the arts, but in welfare and education, was a radical challenge to the way the Foundation saw itself in relation to government:

> We have to recognise that the old, often unspoken partnership between private
> foundations and the public sector, between private initial risk-taking and
> through seed-money which the state then nourishes from permanent resources
> – this partnership is less and less possible. A much greater proportion of
> resources may need to be devoted to sustaining worthwhile projects.

Government or local authority funding was no longer taking over promising new schemes, and worse than that, by 1981, 'high-quality projects faced with extinction have to be supported with crisis grants'. Pressing social needs only served to underline how inadequate the response of the private sector could be when government pulled the rug from under the feet of voluntary organisations. As unemployment rose the Foundation's response was to give grants 'to bodies not only drawing attention to the needs of the unemployed, but also to what action might be taken to overcome them.' In 1982 a large grant of £32,000 was given to set up the Centre for Employment Initiatives (with Peter Kuenstler as one of its directors) as a research and information facility that would promote community enterprise in line with the Foundation's report of that year from Lady Seear, *Community Business Works*, a report that built on the work of *Whose Business is Business?* (1981). The Foundation maintained its interest in community employment by publishing *At the Heart of the Community Economy* in 1993 and *Social Enterprise in Anytown* in 2003.

Self-help and community enterprise were established Foundation themes, and, in response to the new climate of private enterprise, the United Kingdom Branch decided to try to apply what it had learned about

Arts for All. Common Knowledge Theatre's Usk Valley Project, Brecon, 1982. Photo: Common Knowledge Theatre.

self-reliance in its community work to the arts. In 1980 it set up a new programme designed 'to encourage and support self-help initiatives in the arts, comparable to the programme of inner-city self-help', in order 'to discover how [we] can help the arts world to ensure for itself the maintenance of as healthy and flourishing an arts scene as possible in the present circumstances.' In 1979, as Assistant Director, Arts, Ian Lancaster held a series of consultations that led to the formation of the Arts Initiative and Money Project, in which a new advisory committee would fund individual artists and small-scale community and experimental groups, and also initiate its own projects and research. The research was chiefly directed at finding ways to improve the managerial, promotional and financial competence of arts organisations. AIM only ran from 1980 to 1983, and Redmond Mullin's 1984 report for the Foundation makes it clear that the attempt to link artistic experiment with business values was not a success. The advisory committee was an uncomfortable mixture of the arts-minded and business-directed, and it was evident that artists still thought in terms of funding from public sources, rather than private patronage such as the business sponsorship the Conservative government was promoting. Time, and necessity, would change their tune.

In these circumstances it is not surprising that in the 1980 *Annual Report* Brinson should write of the year as one in which:

> all areas of our concern reflected the gloom of the national and international
> situation . . . Major issues are unemployment, housing, health and deteriorating
> community relations; threatened reductions in the quality and range of
> education; the worsening plight of young people, especially young black people,
> and of artists, including those working in education and the community.

Brinson concluded that 'The relative calm of the last twenty-five years is over and huge changes are certain.'

It is possible that this mood was also personal to Brinson, as the political and cultural climate became less and less congenial. In real terms, although its total grants exceeded £1 million for the first time in 1981, the Foundation had less money to spend, and, as it reported in 1982, 'The number of applications increases in every field with every government cut.' At the same time it was experiencing internal change. In 1980 Richard Mills officially retired as Deputy Director (though he stayed on part-time till 1982 and kept closely in touch with Portland Place until his death in 2001), and was succeeded by Paul Curno. In August 1982 Ian Lancaster left as Assistant Director, Arts, in order to pursue his passion for the new technology of holography that he had developed as a result of his work with the Foundation, and was replaced by Iain Reid, a former actor who had become Drama Officer at the Greater London Arts Association. Most important of all was the decision of Sir Charles Whishaw to step down as the Gulbenkian's United Kingdom Trustee in July 1981.

His replacement was Mikhael Essayan, grandson of Calouste Sarkis Gulbenkian, son of Kevork Essayan. Born in 1927, he served in the Royal Artillery, read classics at Balliol and then, out of respect for his grandfather's wishes, worked for the Iraq Petroleum Company in London and the Middle East. But his true interest was the law, which he studied in his spare time, and after his grandfather's death he felt free to be called to the bar in 1957. Although Dr Perdigão had been very reluctant to see Whishaw go, Essayan represented a direct link with the Founder, and he brought a lawyer's urbanity and intellectual precision to the job of linking the United Kingdom Branch to Lisbon. Essayan continued to practise as a barrister until 1988, when he decided that the Foundation needed more time and attention, and remained the United Kingdom Trustee until July 2005.

Essayan took over at a time when there was a certain tension between the administration in Lisbon and the United Kingdom Branch. Now that the Foundation had weathered the storm of the Portuguese revolution, it was felt – as Essayan diplomatically puts it – 'the UK Branch was a little too autonomous'. At the end of 1981 it was decided that the United Kingdom Branch would no longer have responsibility for operations in the Commonwealth, which were taken over by Lisbon, but should continue to conduct activities in the Republic of Ireland. In fact, dealing with the Commonwealth had always been somewhat problematic, for, as Richard Mills wrote later, 'Because of the distances involved it was never possible to make on-the-spot assessments of Commonwealth and South African applications ... One had to rely on a combination of gut feeling and the views of people with first-hand knowledge of particular projects.' Instead of the Commonwealth, the United Kingdom Branch was to launch a new Programme for developing Anglo-Portuguese Cultural Relations, as we will see in chapter five.

Traditional Mekeo dancers at the South Pacific Festival of Arts, Papua New Guinea, 1980. Photo: Office of Information, Port Moresby, Papua New Guinea.

There was also the suggestion from the Trustees that the United Kingdom Branch should be directed by a Portuguese national. This came to nothing, but it became apparent that Brinson was no longer in favour with Lisbon. It was felt that the Foundation was too identified with the London dance scene, and it was unfortunate for Brinson that a scandal should erupt over a grant to a school magazine, *Blot*, which ran an article on sex education that was felt to be unacceptably explicit. It became evident that Brinson's position was no longer tenable and, much to the regret of his staff, in October 1982 he stepped down as Director.

In 1988 Brinson was diagnosed as suffering from myelofribrosis, but he carried on working, including overseeing the report *Arts and Communities* for the Gulbenkian in 1992. He died in 1995. His monument from the Foundation was its publication in 1996 of *Fit to Dance? The report of the national inquiry into dancers' health and injury*. Three years before, in recognition of his services to dance, at the Gulbenkian and elsewhere, he had been presented with the prestigious Digital Dance Award and, with typical generosity, he had given the money to Dance UK, the representative body for the dance profession founded in 1982, to launch the inquiry. He was still working on the report when he died and it was completed by his co-author Fiona Dick, one of the founders of Dance Umbrella, yet another organisation this remarkable man had helped to launch.

Fit to Dance: the first thorough study of dancers' lifestyles, risks and achievements.

CHAPTER 4

Re-building society
1982–1999

'As the word gets round that the public purse is skint, people press upon the foundations and other private sources.'

KIM TAYLOR, *ANNUAL REPORT* 1983–4

This chapter covers the period from the apogee of Thatcherism to the early years of New Labour, from a time when the government was determined to reduce the role of the state to the beginnings of a recasting of collective responsibility. The United Kingdom Branch was faced by a crisis of demand for its funding. It was forced to defend the idea of community and do what it could to alleviate symptoms of deprivation and social alienation, both in inner cities and the countryside. Children and children's rights became a particular concern, while in the arts innovation remained a priority.

OPPOSITE: 'Youth and age in Bethnal Green', from the Urban Studies Centre in East London, which prepared trainee teachers for inner-city schools. Its work is described in *Teachers for the Inner City* by John Raynor, 1981. Photo: Raissa Page.

A New Director

In October 1982 the directorship of the Foundation's United Kingdom Branch was taken over by the 60-year-old L.C. ('Kim') Taylor, who was to stay for six years. Taylor had spent the war in the Indian Army and afterwards studied history at Oxford and adolescent psychology at Chicago. Between 1954 and 1968 Taylor was headmaster of Sevenoaks School, where he gained a reputation as a reformer, introducing such innovations as a Voluntary Service Unit and an International Sixth Form Centre. He then became an educationist, as Director of the Nuffield Foundation's Resources for Learning project (where he wrote a Penguin special of the same name), and then as a Principal Administrator for the Centre for Educational Resources and Innovation at the Organisation for European Co-Operation and Development. At the OECD he became closely involved with education in Portugal – then in a turmoil of reform – as an Examiner for Portugal in their country-by-country review of educational practices. Some years later, his services to education in Portugal were recognised by his being made a Commander of the Order of Prince Henry the Navigator. After leaving the OECD Taylor became Head of Educational Programme Services at the Independent Broadcasting Authority from 1977 to 1982. His knowledge and love of Portugal made him an obvious candidate for the Gulbenkian, but it is clear that there was to be a different approach after Peter Brinson. The London Trustee, Mikhael Essayan, who was still working at the Bar when Taylor took over, remembers him as 'tall, headmasterly, you felt he was an extraordinarily safe pair of hands'.

Iain Reid, who became Assistant Director in charge of Arts shortly before Brinson stepped down, noticed the change of style. He told us: 'Taylor was not an "arts-and-showbiz" person like Brinson. He was extremely well educated and intelligent, and although he was a safe pair of hands, he had a nose for what could be influential, and was prepared to take some big gambles, backed with enough money to make sure projects happened.' Millicent Bowerman confirmed to us that there was a change of pace in the Director's office. 'He was a delight, but a less driven man than Brinson, and he took a more urbane attitude to the job.'

His approach was to lead and help his Assistant Directors, rather than cultivating a separate 'Director's Programme'. He did this by taking on particular projects in all areas of the Branch's work, for example, in Education dealing with the woodworking workshop created by the Parham Trust, and in Social Welfare taking on the Times/RIBA Community Enterprise scheme. He also joined working groups on key reports and gave comments on work-in-progress. The effect of these working methods, together with an open-door policy and a convivial space in which to take refreshment, was to improve integration among the staff and the Programmes.

More conservative in approach than Brinson, Taylor did a great deal to improve the Branch's relationship with Lisbon, and he initiated the Branch's development of a new Anglo-Portuguese Cultural Relations Programme. He was also able to contribute significantly to the Foundation's Education Programme, and to guide and to develop a fruitful relationship with the BBC. As Mikhael Essayan has commented, Kim Taylor's prefaces to the *Annual Report* were 'not intended for hasty and cursory reading. They require and repay careful consideration of the implications of each sentence and at times one may perhaps be reminded of the toils and rewards of reading Proust.' Proustian or not, Taylor had no hesitation in protesting against the damage he felt Thatcherism was doing to the arts and social services through its changes to local government – the area that affected the Foundation's work most.

He also used the pages of the *Annual Report* to meditate on the appropriate policies and functions for private foundations in the rapidly changing

Woodcut by Franz Cizek. One of the items in the National Arts Education Archive at Bretton Hall, University of Leeds, which received a grant in 1986 towards development costs. By kind permission of Wanda Stanley.

An artwork created with children in Brighton by Same Sky, an arts education agency, which in 1998 established a scheme to facilitate contact between teachers and local artists willing to work in schools. Photo: John Varah.

Young people taking part in a Community Dance Week organised by the Dundee Repertory Dance Company, 1986. Photo: Ian Southern.

political and social climate. In order to clarify its advice to applicants, the 1984 report carried the first fold-out *Advice to Applicants for Grants* leaflet outlining the Foundation's redefined priorities: in the Arts, to make them more accessible for a wider public, especially for multicultural or ethnic minority projects, plus development and training for experienced artists and the encouragement of overseas contacts; in Education, a complementary emphasis on arts for young people, together with educational innovation, and a strand aimed at bringing archives into better educational use by encouraging the appointment of museum education officers; in Social Welfare, neighbourhood work initiatives, neighbourhood care and support services for local groups.

Taylor had to face the continuing problem of a fall in the real value of the Foundation's resources, at a time when demand was increasing as the state drew back. The pattern of grant-giving had to change in the face of the pressures that grant applicants were experiencing. The general policy that grants should be a maximum of £10,000 (then the limit before agreement had to be obtained from Lisbon) conflicted with the need to encourage stability and sustainability for grant recipients, and when the basic operating costs of organisations were no longer funded by government, there were pleas to the Foundation to step in. Paul Curno described to us 'a mountain of applications suddenly received from playgroups and old people's groups', people who had never been in touch with the Gulbenkian before, and who were casting about in an attempt to survive. In 1984 the Social Welfare budget made a number of grants to cover administration costs and the Foundation funded the salaries of a national co-ordinator for Church Action with the Unemployed, a neighbourhood worker for the Leeds Council for Voluntary Service, and workers at both Powys Self-Help and Youth Education Service, Bristol.

The Foundation had always been a fervent believer in self-help, and in an odd way, there was some consonance in the language used by the Foundation and the government. But the differences are more important. The Foundation understood that people needed help in order to help themselves, whereas the government was content simply to abandon responsibility. When, for example, a single-industry town lost its main source of employment, the reaction of ministers was either to exhort people to get on their bikes and look for work, or to use a centralist planning model such as Urban Development Agencies to urge big business to invest. The

Roots and Shoots, a woodwork project at Lady Margaret Hall Settlement, Lambeth, in the early 1980s, to improve employment opportunities for students with special educational needs. Photo: LMHS.

Foundation's response was to help the community to organise itself, and for people to assist each other. In 1983 the Foundation funded twenty-one local employment initiatives, most of which were based on principles of community, mutuality and co-operation.

The government saw every solution lying at the level of the individual operating in a free market: reduce public spending so as to give people more for themselves, give people choice through expanding the role of the private sector. For a Foundation dedicated to the improvement of society, it was a challenge to operate in a climate where the Prime Minister took the view, as she told *Woman's Own* in October 1987, that 'There is no such thing as society, only individual men and women and their families.'

Taylor was appalled at the government's attitude. Apologists often used the analogy of Darwinianism to explain official policies, but Taylor argued in 1984 that 'It is modern catastrophe theory, with its emphasis on the sudden and haphazard, not Darwinian evolution, with its gently adaptive survival of the fittest, that provides the better analogy for the effects of the radical policy shifts in our time.' He had in mind such random events as the local government Council of the Western Isles in Scotland suddenly losing most of its money due to the collapse of the BCCI bank. But he was also thinking about deliberate government actions such as rate-capping and the abolition of the Metropolitan County Councils that emasculated local government and put nothing in its place. It was, he said, 'enough to cast a black, black shadow before. The prospects look bleak.'

There was no doubt that government policies hurt. Researchers at the University of Bristol commented in *Meaningful Statistics on Poverty*, 1991: 'Trends in income in the 1980s represent a disaster for the poor.' Between 1979 and 1989 the proportion of households with incomes below 50 per cent of the average increased from 7 to 19 per cent. This might not have mattered if everyone was getting better off, but they were not. In the same period, the bottom 10 per cent of households saw their real disposable income fall by 5 per cent, while the top 10 per cent saw theirs rise by 30 per cent. Within these grim statistics, the increase in child poverty was of particular concern to the Foundation. Such was the social revolution engendered by Thatcherism that the increase in social inequality and child poverty was not to begin to level out, let alone fall, until the beginning of a new century.

145

Local Government Reorganisation

The reorganisation – in fact diminution – of local government had drastic implications for the Foundation. The effect of the Conservatives' Local Government Act of 1972 had been benign. Local authorities had been re-organised into a two-tier system of county and district councils, but in addition the six main centres of population – Manchester, Merseyside, South Yorkshire, Tyneside, the West Midlands and West Yorkshire – were grouped as Metropolitan County Councils, giving them the economic and political clout of the Greater London Council, created in 1965. The GLC and the MCCs had the resources to drive their own social and cultural policies. In 1981, led by Ken Livingstone, the GLC began to develop a new cultural strategy that owed a great deal to the principles of the community arts movement, and for a time local authority arts funding prospered generally. But the GLC and the MCCs were Labour-dominated, and represented an alternative source of power and practice to that of Mrs Thatcher's government. In 1984 Taylor warned in the *Annual Report*: 'The austerities of 1983 are now to be reinforced by rate-capping and the suppression of the metropolitan councils. The loss of the metropolitan tier of administration puts the arts especially at risk.' The Arts Council tried to avert this crisis by proposing a restructuring of its responsibilities in its 1984 policy document *The Glory of the Garden*, but the government failed to respond with sufficiently increased resources. After a long period of protest, in 1986 the GLC and its fellow MCCs were abolished, and the national arts funding system was thrown into chaos as the Arts Council tried to pick up the pieces as best it could.

Although the Foundation had to keep out of party politics, strong opinions were expressed about what Taylor saw as a breach of contract by government as it bore down on public expenditure: 'The image convention-ally used to describe development grants given by foundations like this one has been "pump-priming",' he wrote in 1986. 'That assumes the existence of ample water in a known well. A rising proportion of our grants are now for "tanking up", to keep the recipients alive while they wander in arid regions.' After introducing rate-capping in 1985, in 1988 the government introduced a fresh Local Government Finance Act to abolish local taxation through the rating system and replace it with the Poll Tax, which came into force in Scotland in 1989 and England and Wales in 1990. At the same time local

Bradford Council for Voluntary Service oversaw the rehabilitation of a historic Bradford square inhabited by a close-knit Pakistani community, 1983. Photo: Reproduced by kind permission of the *Telegraph & Argus*, Bradford.

authorities' major services were opened up to competitive tendering. This meant that whole swathes of local authority provision, from parks and swimming pools to housing and care services, were no longer directly provided but were 'contracted out'.

At first sight the changes heralded by the 1988 Act looked ominous for the voluntary sector: a National Council for Voluntary Organisations survey showed that local authorities chopped their funding to the voluntary sector in England and Wales by at least £29.4 million in 1991, and even more severe cuts totalling £42.4 million were expected in 1992/3. But competitive tendering had a consequence that perhaps had not been intended in the rush to privatisation: 'It seems obvious that the government in fact needs the voluntary sector more than vice versa,' commented the 1989 *Annual Report*. In the space of a few years, the voluntary sector changed. It no longer performed merely an important, but peripheral, charitable role; rather it became a major provider of 'government' services. With that came public money, public accountability, and a renewed interest on the part of politicians, who might now be judged on the performance of these 'third-sector' service providers. Public-sector funding shifted from being in the form of grants to being tied to 'deliverables'. In the process there were big winners and losers. But in the early 1990s some charities began to receive large-scale funding so that they could manage services formerly provided directly by the state.

In an attempt to help the voluntary sector to understand the threats and opportunities that now lay open to them, the Foundation funded the Voluntary Sector Working Group on Contracting Out to organise bulletins, publications, conferences and workshops around the country to fathom what it all might mean. It also helped Richard Gutch, former Chief Executive of Arthritis Care, to travel to the United States to research his 1991 report *Contracting in the USA*. All this was done in something of a hurry, in the wake of the legislation. Better preparations were made in 1989 when, three years ahead of the implementation of the Single European Market, a grant was given to the Community Projects Foundation to prepare a guide to the opportunities, resources and networks in Europe and the effects the Single European Market would have on community organisations.

Education: 'the Year of the Gerbil
– the Great Education Reform Bill'

During his time as Director, Kim Taylor had to deal with the consequences of 'the great debate' about education launched by Labour's Prime Minister Jim Callaghan in 1976, and with the introduction of the National Curriculum by the Education Reform Act of 1988, the year of Taylor's retirement. It was a matter of particular concern to the Foundation that the National Curriculum developed into a highly restrictive programme that focused on certain subjects such as maths, English and the sciences. Whatever the intention, the practical effect was to push art and music to the periphery, and also to restrict the ways in which the core subjects were taught. Faced with these issues, and the need to protect aspects of education both within and beyond schools, Taylor decided to revive the post of Assistant Director, Education, dropped by Brinson, and appointed Simon Richey in June 1984. Like many Foundation staff, Richey's background was sufficiently eclectic to provide all the right ingredients for the task. He had spent time teaching at secondary level, had worked for the BBC and had been a youth worker for the National Association of Boys' Clubs, and in that role had been engaged in the arts.

When Richey arrived, the major part of the Education Programme's budget was being spent on 'Educational Disadvantage, age 14–25'. The term 'disadvantage' covered a wide field, giving support to the young unemployed, ethnic minorities, the handicapped and the deprived. Unusually for that time, the Foundation also perceived that the gifted and talented were in a particular way disadvantaged, in that many found themselves unable to realise their full potential. Consequently, a small corner of the portfolio was devoted to what Mikhael Essayan jokingly suggested calling 'the severely gifted'. The second area of focus was on 'The Educational Use of Archives'. With the reinvigoration of education that Taylor and Richey together provided, new priorities were adopted: 'Educational Innovations and Developments' and 'Arts for Young People', although support for archives continued on a modest scale for a few more years. 'Educational Innovation' gave the Foundation the flexibility to pursue its long-held role of funding pioneering and unusual initiatives such as helping the Small School, an

Conductor Simon Rattle leads a workshop in a Birmingham primary school as part of the City of Birmingham Symphony Orchestra's Adopt-a-Player Scheme, 1987. Photo: Birmingham Post and Mail.

Teacher and pupils outside a school in Scoraig, North-West Scotland, established by parents and built by local volunteers. Photo: Denis Thorpe. © Guardian Newspapers Limited 1989.

ecologically focused secondary school in rural North Devon, and allowing the Scottish Civil Liberty Trust to test and disseminate learning materials about the law in relation to everyday matters.

Taylor considered education to be 'a nebulous, complex, individual and uncertain matter', and concluded that the Foundation should direct its attention beyond that 'limited range of issues suited to rational, public discourse'. As he says, 'Young people learn to protect themselves from the official education blazed at them by a mist of self-absorption, forgetfulness and dreams, and do most of their real growing more obscurely, by moonlight, like plants, and by moonlighting.' This sentiment manifested itself in an increasing concern with the emotional health of children, and the first steps were taken to address both help-line availability and the issue of playground bullying; but more immediately the Foundation saw the arts as creating an important space for young people outside the common path of the curriculum, and indeed outside school.

Following its publication of *The Arts in Schools* in 1982 the Foundation began to concentrate on a different age group, early childhood to 18 rather than 14 to 25, and all sorts of activities were supported, from traditional arts-in-education projects such as the Kosh Dance Theatre Company doing school workshops, through a grant to a group of young people in Birmingham who wanted to run their own arts festival, to funding a 'pop group in residence' in Coventry. A wide variety of art forms was supported, including poetry and circus, although it is fair to say that music, dance and theatre predominated. But the Foundation was troubled by the position of the arts outside school, recognising that 'once the compulsion exercised by a school ceases, most young people have little to do with the arts'. One consequence was the decision to encourage the arts in Youth Services as well as in schools; another was to set up an enquiry into the place of the popular and personal arts in the lives of young people beyond the curriculum – a complementary work to Robinson's *The Arts in Schools*. The report, by Paul Willis, was published by the Foundation in 1990 as *Moving Culture*. A revised text was published by Open University Press as *Common Culture*.

Art: 'the Big Idea'

The values of communal self-expression, popular art forms and localised activity that had driven the United Kingdom Branch's commitment to community art in the 1970s (and which had their roots in the non-metropolitan attitude of the Bridges Report) continued to shape the policy of the Arts Department, although somewhat recast as 'access' in order to complement the Education Department's 'Arts for Young People' programme. In 1983 there were important grants to help set up a new organisation, Arts for Disabled People in Wales, and help with training for Graeae Theatre Company, which continues to be Britain's only theatre company of disabled actors. Most of the 'access' strand of activities was handed over entirely to Education in 1986, but the Arts Department retained a significant commitment to the legacy of *The Arts Britain Ignores* by supporting ethnic arts. By 1987 it was devoting 25 per cent of its departmental budget to help support organisations such as the Asian theatre company Tara Arts, the West Midlands Ethnic Minority Arts Advisory Service, the ethnic arts development programme of Yorkshire Arts, the Theatre of Black Women and the Black Theatre Co-Operative. Carrying on the Brinson tradition of support for dance, there was a major commitment to black and Asian dance, with support for the Academy of Indian Dance in 1985, and the first-ever

Back to Front with Sideshows, 1994. CandoCo Dance Company, which gave masterclasses and workshops in Ireland on how to work with disabled dancers. Photo: Anthony Crickmay.

Dance Exchange/Dancers of the Third Age from Washington DC lead a workshop during Dance Umbrella 1988. Photo: Lois Greenfield.

National Black Dance School launched at Leicester Polytechnic in 1986, the same year that new black dance companies Adzido and Irie started up with Foundation help. The Black Dance Development Trust was established in 1987 and Kokuma dance company funded in 1988.

The shift of the general 'access' programme to Education meant that more emphasis could be given to artists' training, which was being neglected

Adzido, Pan African Dance Ensemble, a touring company of musicians and dancers from twelve countries, 1987. Photo: Tim Jarvis.

153

'Sidesaddle Samba'.
Circus Senso
performing at the
Albany Empire, 1985.
Photo: Sarah Ainslie.

by public funding bodies as they struggled to keep companies performing. The switch in resources was from 17 per cent of the Arts budget in 1985 to 45 per cent in 1988. In 1989 the Foundation published *A Better Direction*, the result of a year-long enquiry into the training for directors in theatre, film and television, which led to the timely renewal of the Arts Council's diminishing training scheme. The Foundation invested in an extension of this scheme and was joined by the Esmée Fairbairn Foundation, which took up the baton when the Foundation finally withdrew.

Investment was also made in the then unrecognised art form of 'new circus'. As Iain Reid wrote in 1985, this was 'far removed from the tawdry image of the sawdust ring'. He saw it 'as a tool for arts in education and in the community, and as an art in its own right, developing in some countries fast, but still at an early stage here.' There was a link back to the world of community art, for the idea of promoting new circus was brought to the Foundation by Reg Bolton, who had established his Suitcase Circus with the Craigmillar Festival Society. Bolton was funded to research and write *New Circus*, published by the Foundation in 1987. In 1985 workshops at the Albany – another long-standing friend of the United Kingdom Branch – led to the creation of Circus Senso, and in 1987 a start-up grant went to Fool Time in Bristol, the first-ever training school for circus skills in Britain. Fool

Il Ladro Di Anime (Thief of Souls), La Gaia Scienza, Italy. Georgio Barberio Corsetti's dance theatre production at LIFT'85. Photo: Courtesy of LIFT archive.

Time is now known as Circomedia, and circus has since been recognised as an art form by the Arts Council and the National Endowment for Science, Technology and the Arts (NESTA).

The revival of the old physical skills of circus went with the exploration of the new technical possibilities of video. Money was made available for video workshops, and in 1986 the Arts Department backed a major experiment in television technique by giving Dance Umbrella £22,000 towards the cost of preparatory camera and dance research for Channel Four television's *Dance-lines* commission. Previously, dance performances had been recorded in a very static manner, now cameramen were taught how to work with dancers, and the dancers how to work with the camera. The Foundation created a new Dance Awards Scheme, using it to help commission foreign choreographers as part of its policy of encouraging contact with international influences. The London International Festival of Theatre, founded in 1981 at a time when there was very little opportunity to see foreign drama in London, let alone the experimental work favoured by its founders Lucy Neal and Rose Fenton, began to receive Foundation support for its biennial programmes. (The Foundation's support for LIFT has recently culminated in the publication of *The Turning World: Stories from the London International Festival of Theatre*, 2005.)

A student from Edinburgh College of Art at the Scottish Sculpture Workshop, Aberdeenshire, which received a grant of £10,000 in 1983. Photo: Andy Dewar.

As Iain Reid described it to us, it was the Foundation's practice 'to have our antennae out, looking for what was bubbling'. This process led the Foundation in 1983 into a new field of arts activity where the practice of a 'high' art – principally sculpture – could find a new and more democratic context and be enjoyed by as many people as possible. This new Public Art was a response to a general sense of decay in the public realm, and an area where the Foundation could act as a catalyst, funding infrastructure rather than directly commissioning works of art, first of all by helping new agencies such as the Public Arts Development Trust and the Artists' Agency in Sunderland, and then supporting imaginative schemes such as the Oxford Sculpture Project (creating works in schools), the Scottish Sculpture Workshop, the Welsh Sculpture Trust and Common Ground's New Milestone project, to encourage new art commissions in local settings. There was also help to the Royal College of Art to launch a new course in environmental and landscape sculpture.

The range of these projects, from milestones to earthworks to forest trails, shows that as Reid wrote in the *Annual Report* in 1987, the Foundation conceived of Public Art as a great deal more than:

> the lump of stone in the plaza. Its definition should include the work of artists
> in designing colour schemes or signs in hospitals, in collaborating with
> architects to produce better-looking buildings, in working with town planners
> on the design of street furniture, and so on.

The Foundation therefore developed relationships with housing trusts and health authorities that wanted to improve their local environment. In 1987 it helped Manchester Polytechnic establish a centre to promote research and training in the provision of arts in health-care buildings, Health Care Arts. The Director was Peter Senior, who back in 1976 had been able to support his pioneering work as 'hospital artist' at St Mary's Hospital in Manchester by becoming a Gulbenkian artist-in-the-community. The Foundation recorded Senior's work and ideas in Peter Coles's *Manchester*

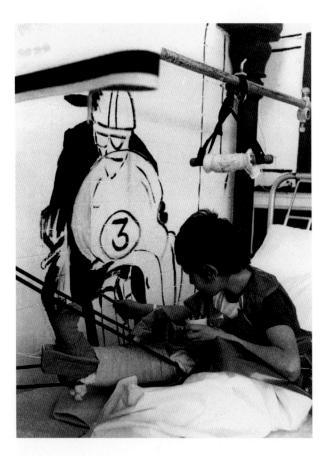

Painting a mural at
St Mary's Hospital,
Manchester, from
*Manchester Hospital's
Arts Project* by Peter
Coles, 1981.
Photo: Brian Chapman.

Hospitals' Arts Project in 1981, and Senior and Jonathan Croall's *Helping to Heal* in 1993. A further intervention in arts and health came in the form of support for art in hospices. This was an idea from the fertile mind of the extraordinarily inventive social entrepreneur Michael Young (later Lord Young of Dartington), and only one of the many occasions on which he and the Foundation worked together.

A similar willingness to respond to what the Foundation's antennae were picking up led to the development of what became known in Portland Place as 'The Big Idea' – the Foundation's Large-Scale Events Scheme. At a time when the limitations of arts funding were shrinking ambitions and narrowing horizons, it was felt that there was a need for a grand gesture, a performance or event of the kind that was taking place at festivals in Europe, but which seemed beyond the capacities of British funders. Such events, which used mixed media, were unable to tour and had few performances, were almost designed to fail the usual criteria for public funding. Michael Morris, then running the theatre at the Institute of Contemporary Arts, and now a Co-Director of Artangel, approached Iain Reid with a proposal. A group of experts was put together, and in 1987 it was decided to set aside £60,000 for a scheme to promote large-scale events in specific environments – public art and public spectacle. £15,000 was made available for selected artists or teams to research and develop their schemes, of which three would go into production, sharing £45,000 between them. No fewer than 299 projects were submitted, revealing an untapped well of ideas and ambition. A group called Emergency Exit Arts wanted to turn the demolition of a block of council flats into a performance, and demonstrated their plans by blowing up a scale model on the Foundation's boardroom table; another group designed a travelling performance piece linking London's abandoned Underground stations. Fourteen projects went into development in 1988, of which the three chosen were a gigantic scrap and firework sculpture in

Golden Submarine, **Welfare State International, Barrow-in-Furness, 1990. Photo: Ged Murray.**

Barrow-in-Furness by the town's resident artists Welfare State (old friends of the Foundation), Ann Wilson and Marty St James's open-air performance piece *Civic Monument*, and the sculptor George Wyllie's enormous paper boat, which graced the Clyde during Glasgow's year as Capital of Culture in 1990, and sailed both on the Thames and the Hudson. The Arts Department could claim both to have thought, and acted, big.

Community Work, Unemployment and Big Business

In 1981 the Foundation published *Whose Business is Business?*, a report of a working party set up by the Foundation and the Manpower Services Commission in partnership with Shell, GEC and the National Westminster Bank. The report investigated existing community business ventures and the potential for new local economic enterprise, and gave rise to fresh thinking about how local economic development might be stimulated. It was followed up in 1982 with the publication of *Community Business Works*, the report of a committee chaired by Baroness Seear who was also Chair of the House of Lords Committee on Employment. Community business became an important theme for the Foundation. In 1982 Paul Curno undertook a research trip to the United States, visiting a dozen cities and returning, he told us, 'immensely inspired' by the examples of work that he had seen. He also came across the idea of community foundations, where individuals and companies pay money into an endowment fund for a local area. The Gulbenkian helped fund such a venture in South Yorkshire in 1982, and the idea was further developed by the Charities Aid Foundation in the mid-1980s, and by the Esmée Fairbairn Foundation in 2000, so that there are now sixty thriving community foundations around the country, with Tyne and Wear providing perhaps the most vibrant example. Collectively, they hold an estimated £100 million in assets and allocated £53 million to community groups in 2004.

A further major outcome of the US visit was an invitation to Mike Sviridoff, the President of the US organisation Local Initiatives Support Corporation, to tour a number of UK cities in order to spread the word about how local collaborations between business and the voluntary sector could revitalise local economies and neighbourhoods. The exchange, however, was not all one way. Sviridoff's visit to Govan Workspace led to the importation of the workspace concept to the United States.

Although not directly resulting from the Gulbenkian's initiatives in community business, the publications and conferences did feed into the establishment in 1981 of Business in the Community, whose second meeting was hosted by the Foundation. Indeed the Foundation was helpful in acting as a bridge between BITC and the voluntary sector, which was not always easy. David Thomas comments that 'The [Sviridoff] visit was ahead of its time for the UK', and one reason for this is that government thinking was flowing in the opposite direction. Indifference to community enterprise when James Prior was Secretary of State for Unemployment changed to outright hostility when Norman Tebbit took over the job.

Undaunted, the Foundation funded a conference in 1984, together with the Stock Exchange and Business in the Community, to bring together City institutions, industry and representatives of local government and the voluntary sector, to try to find ways of meeting the needs of the long-term unemployed. But the Foundation's relationship with big business has always been equivocal. There have been few collaborations between the Foundation and the business sector, and the involvement of leading business figures has been the exception, not the rule.

Perhaps this is because of business's own lack of philanthropic engagement. In 1989 corporate profits hit a historic peak of 13.4 per cent, but corporate charitable giving declined in real terms, while the proportion of pre-tax profit donated remained static at a meagre 0.2 per cent throughout the decade. The corporate sector's parsimony, in both absolute and relative terms (the proportion of pre-tax profit donated in the US in the 1980s averaged 1.9 per cent) was often explained as legally and morally right: corporate giving was a theft from the shareholders, and it was up to newly enriched individuals, who had seen their personal tax bills tumble, to act with generosity to fill the gap. In November 1991 John Major appealed to the public, and particularly to wealthy entrepreneurs: 'Everyone can give . . . we want to see more grant-making trusts set up in the 1990s.' Unfortunately, as the Branch's *Annual Report* noted, individual giving declined: 'Both the proportion of members of the public who give to charity, and the per capita amount they give in the UK, are at present falling.' And, barring a few honourable exceptions, John Major's words fell on stony ground. The rich continued to give a lower proportion of their income than the poor and only a handful of significant new grant-making trusts was established.

The Economic Importance of the Arts

In 1984, in response to the increasing threat to public funding of the arts, the Foundation initiated the production of a report that was to be as significant in its time as the Bridges and Redcliffe-Maud Reports before it. In the face of the cash-driven ideology of Thatcherism the arts had to prove that they were more than just a good thing – they had to be value for money. Iain Reid decided to investigate. As he told us: 'I thought this was something the Arts Council should be interested in, so I approached them offering a joint project – and got no response. So we went off and did it.'

Stella Smith working at the Priory Garage during her placement with the North East Co-op, Gateshead. The Foundation's 1986 publication *What the hell do we want an artist here for?* examined artists-in-industry placements from the standpoints of the companies, artists and arts administrators involved. Photo: Keith Patterson.

Having secured the co-operation of the government's Office of Arts and Libraries, Reid commissioned the independent Policy Studies Institute to undertake the most ambitious research project ever undertaken into the arts. The Foundation's launch grant was £45,000 (with a further £17,500 to come), and by the time *The Economic Importance of the Arts in Britain* was published in 1988, not only the Arts Council, but the Museums and Galleries Commission, and the Crafts Council, together with a dozen local and regional bodies, had joined in a project that might, in some sense, ensure their survival. In 1989 the Foundation made a further grant of £30,000 to disseminate the conclusions of the report.

The research was led by the cultural economist John Myerscough, and appeared in four volumes. The first three were detailed regional studies: Merseyside, where the imminent abolition of the Merseyside Metropolitan Council made a study urgent; Glasgow, desperately in need of regeneration in the wake of the city's industrial decline; and, for comparison, a study of the more rural setting of Ipswich. The information from these studies fed into the final volume assessing the cultural economy of the country as a whole.

This was the first time that the now familiar claims for the economic contribution of the arts were properly articulated. The basic conclusion was that the sector had:

> A turnover of £10 billion, amounting to 2.5 per cent of all goods and services by UK residents and foreign buyers, and giving employment to almost half a million people ... the arts are placed fourth among the top ten invisible export earners. Public funding ... represents 18 per cent of income for the sectors; the balance is shifting from central government to local authorities and from public funding to private finance. The large element of small businesses in the sector makes it a seedbed for future growth and a place for research and development.

Twenty-seven per cent of overseas earnings were specifically attributable to the arts. In total, the 'cultural industries' – a new and significant term – contributed 1.28 per cent of gross domestic product, making the arts roughly equivalent in importance to the (declining) motor industry.

The report stressed the common European aspect of this approach to the arts. All over Europe, central government spending on the arts had been tailing off, and arguments for their support based on their educational value or intrinsic worth had lost their force. The purely economic value of the arts had seemed a potentially persuasive argument, but Myerscough wanted to take this further:

> In retrospect, the early 1980s' stress on the economic value of the arts reads like special pleading by those defending the arts against threatened reductions in public spending. It was set in no particular policy frame and might have applied equally to any area of public spending, to defence as much as to drama companies. In the space of a few years, the argument has moved on to higher ground, by relating the role of the arts to the fact that we live in an era of industrial restructuring characterised by the growing importance of the service industries (especially in the areas of finance, knowledge, travel and entertain- ment), and of industries based on new technologies exploiting information and the media.

To make this point, Myerscough developed arguments about the 'multiplier effect' of arts spending, to show how indirect spending and employment was generated by direct spending on the arts. He ended on a note of 'national prestige and value to the public':

> It is an important conclusion of this report that the arts sector is capable of great expansion which will benefit the economy. It is an even more significant fact that this will increase the artistic experience of the British people for present and future generations.

This was welcome news to the sponsors of the report. Iain Reid wrote in the 1988 *Annual Report*: 'The main thrust of the PSI report's argument is that it is the social and aesthetic value of the arts which makes them economically so successful. It is also important to recognise the complex web of connections which exist within the arts sector between commercial enterprises, education, training and artistic experiment. It is short-sighted to point out the success of the non-subsidised music industry without accepting the need to finance music lessons in primary school or to support the community music projects which feed and underpin the industry.'

It is fair to say that the economic theory underpinning the report was challenged. Myerscough's multiplier effect was questioned, as was the effec- tiveness of the arts as job-creators, and it was argued that the additional consumer spending on the arts was only an internal shift of resources from one area of the economy to another. It was also pointed out that out of the grand total of £10 billion, perhaps only 10 per cent was generated by conventional arts activities. But that was partly the point: the 'arts' were now part of a wider phenomenon, the 'cultural industries'. The spread of this term was to have a profound effect on public policy right into the next century. The argument was immediately taken up by local authorities seeking ways to regenerate their towns and cities through heritage projects and cultural tourism. It is a sign of the economic importance of *The Economic Importance of the Arts in Britain* that, in the market for reports, it became a best seller.

Ireland

Taylor took a particular interest, and was personally considerably involved, in developing the United Kingdom Branch's Programme for the Republic of Ireland. The Republic remained a responsibility of London when management of British Commonwealth projects returned to Lisbon in 1982, and a distinct strand of work there was launched in 1985. Taylor realised that it was best to collaborate with Irish bodies who had local and expert knowledge, so at first, sums of around £100,000 a year were channelled through two

A Groundwork Northern Ireland project in the North Belfast estate of Mount Vernon, where twenty-five young people worked with a local artist on a community mural to cover graffiti, 1999. Photo: Dianne McGill.

Coastwatch volunteers help to survey and clean up a section of Ireland's coastline, 1993. Photo: Coastwatch Europe.

organisations, ACE (Arts Community Education – an Irish Arts Council project to develop community arts in Ireland) and the Irish Heritage Trust, which directed the money towards environmental conservation projects rather than the built heritage. The new Programme quickly flourished, with the Irish government or Irish organisations often committing much larger funding than the Foundation's own.

Ben Whitaker

In October 1988, following Kim Taylor's retirement, his place was taken by the 54-year-old former barrister Ben Whitaker, who had been MP for Hampstead from 1966 to 1970, and a junior minister in Harold Wilson's government. He then became Director of the Minority Rights Group and had written an independent study of the role and effects of philanthropic foundations in society throughout the world. He told us that he was 'surprised to be appointed', as his expertise was in human rights; Mikhael

Essayan, however, told us he was 'rather attracted to the idea of an old Etonian Labour MP – I thought he should be pretty balanced.' Like Peter Brinson before him, Whitaker understood the value of keeping a good table where he could entertain the Great and the Good. Whitaker had a taste for cartoons, and for the next twelve years the *Annual Report* is regularly enlivened by the work of Posy Simmonds, H.M. Bateman and others. Indeed, the reports take on a lighter, chattier, tone. Whitaker's comments were headed 'From the Rostrum', or 'From the Pulpit', dusted with quotations, and even contained jokes, such as 'My tiny funds are frozen.'

Whitaker stayed as Director until 1999, witnessing the change from John Major to New Labour. He had a different style from the avuncular Kim Taylor, insisting on joint meetings because 'we were all really working in isolation and some good projects are multi-departmental'. At the same time he introduced the category of discretionary 'Director's Grants', based on the argument that the Foundation should be taking more initiatives and encouraging applications instead of just responding to them. As these grants came out of existing departmental allocations, the policy was not popular with his Assistant Directors. Iain Reid became unhappy with Whitaker's somewhat contrarian style, and in 1989 left to join the Arts Council, where he was put in charge of Combined Arts, the field of experimental and mixed-media art forms and performance. As he told us, 'What I had learned at the Gulbenkian about investing in the research and development phase of a project before going ahead I was able to apply and develop at the Arts Council.'

Whitaker emphasised the Branch's policy of funding as much as possible away from London and the South-East, and encouraged his staff to travel. The principle was for each of the three Departments to have three themes in hand at any one time: a main theme, one in development, and one winding down. He decided to pull back from Taylor's policy of being willing to risk quite large sums on certain projects, preferring to keep to the £10,000 limit to any single grant, beyond which authorisation from Lisbon was necessary. This was partly to preserve funds, for by 1989 inflation and exchange-rate changes meant that there was increasing pressure on resources (225 grants were given that year – and 1,917 applications rejected). He also decided not to fund so many conferences and seminars but instead to put resources more directly into tackling social problems. However, the Foundation wanted to do this without replacing money lost through government cuts.

In order to ensure that the Foundation was getting value for money, applicants were encouraged to evaluate the results of their completed projects properly, and sums began to be built into budgets for a post-project evaluation. Whitaker told us: 'We were never sure precisely what effect our grants had, and I considered setting up a separate evaluation unit.' The money was given for independent evaluations, and Whitaker says he 'rather welcomed negative findings, for their honesty. That way the project would benefit by learning lessons as well as us. I always used to give them extra marks.' In 1996 the Foundation funded David N. Thomas's *Oil on Troubled Waters: The Gulbenkian Foundation and social welfare*, a thorough evaluation and statistical survey of the United Kingdom Branch's welfare policies between 1965 and 1990 that we have cited several times.

Whitaker appears to have become increasingly suspicious of some of those asking for money. He commented in the 1991 *Annual Report*: 'One cannot work for many days as a grant-giver before realising that those people who write the most skilful applications are not necessarily – indeed probably are rarely – the same people who are doing the most worthwhile charitable work.' Evidently irritated by the voluntary sector's tendency to use pseudo-managerial business language with relish, the following year he reprinted verbatim an application from an unnamed charity:

> This stage will end immediately prior to the customisation and implementation
> of the model and the deliverable will be the draft generic model and implemen-
> tation plans for pilot locations. It is also intended to identify during this phase
> and from the outcome of the national seminar in Phase 1, one or more
> potential national-level partners for the national 'role-out' [sic] after the next
> phase ... the widespread uptake of the model, using the 'tool-kit' and an
> increasing network of training consultants is the next target. This will be an
> extended process and very much market driven from among the varying
> interests and motivations of the potential locales ...

The application was unsuccessful.

In dealings with the Republic of Ireland, Whitaker changed the Branch's policy, preferring to offer grants directly, in what amounted to a smaller version of the United Kingdom model, and mirroring many of its concerns, from children's rights to an annual award for museums, launched in 1992. He told us: 'The needs in Ireland were enormous, and there were almost no

167

foundations willing to work there. One or two grants really broke ground, especially cross-border initiatives during those difficult times.' Whitaker's reports on the Programme regularly closed with the comment that Ireland's needs were great, and offering to give help or advice to any foundation that was considering entering the field.

Walter Segal
Self Build Trust's
cross-border project
trained communities
in both parts of
Ireland to build their
own homes, 1999.
Photo: WSSBT.

Children

One of the areas of concern that Whitaker inherited from Kim Taylor was that of children's lives and children's rights. The situation of many children had worsened throughout the 1980s and into the 1990s; inequality in earnings in 1994 was greater than at any time since records were first kept in 1886, and one consequence was that one in three children was growing up in poverty. In turn, poverty bred crime, ignorance and despair. In 1991, Scotland had 16,769 crimes per 100,000 population, while Portugal had 712. In 1994, one in seven 21-year-olds had difficulty with basic reading.

The Foundation had long sought to address the needs of children but in the middle of the decade four major grants for research and policy material indicate a sharp increase in interest in the subject. Paul Curno had spotted a 'gap in the market', and had also found in Peter Newell 'a guru behind all the thinking'. Newell acted as an adviser to the Foundation for the next ten years, and in 1989 children's rights became a declared priority, perhaps also reflecting Whitaker's professional interest in human rights.

1989 saw the passage of the Children's Act and also the signing of the United Nations Convention on the Rights of the Child, which provided a framework for promoting children's rights. In 1990 the Foundation was instrumental in setting up the Children's Rights Development Unit with a grant of £45,000, and with Gerison Lansdown as its first Director. This new independent body was needed in order to embed children's rights in the voluntary sector and in government, helping both voluntary and statutory agencies implement the Convention. One of its first priorities was to draw up the *UK Agenda for Children*, which was endorsed by 180 organisations. This detailed, comprehensive and compelling document, written by Lansdown and Newell, mapped existing legislation, policy and practice against the UN Convention, and recommended changes to bring the UK into line.

The Foundation also commissioned and published, in 1991, a report entitled *Taking Children Seriously: A proposal for a Children's Rights Commissioner* that called for an Ombudsman for children and contained a draft bill to implement the idea. Despite repeated calls by the Foundation and all the main children's charities, nothing happened, and progress was slow. After four years, Ben Whitaker commented: 'Sadly, so far there has been little action on the part of the UK government to translate these global aspirations (i.e. those of the UN Convention) into active policies which have any meaning at a national level, let alone at community, neighbourhood or family level.' The road that the Foundation had started upon was to be a long one, but eventually in June 2003 the first Minister for Children was appointed, with sole responsibility for issues affecting children. By July 2005 England and the devolved governments of Scotland, Wales, and Northern Ireland had all appointed Children's Commissioners. The increasing coherence in government policy about children's issues was in part the result of another Gulbenkian report, co-authored by Rachel Hodgkin and Peter Newell, called *Effective Government Structures for Children*, that surveyed the ways in which public services met the needs of the country's 13 million under-18s. The report came out in December 1996, well timed to catch the attention of an incoming Labour government in May 1997. The publication was backed by a large and powerful committee, chaired by Sir Peter Newsam (former Chair of the Commission for Racial Equality) and including Peter Mandelson MP, Sir Stephen Tumin (former Chief Inspector of Prisons) and the child psychologist Dr Penelope Leach.

While the mechanisms of government moved slowly, the Foundation did what it could, in the form of grants, to find out more about children's needs wherever they were in distress. How could children find a voice when families were splitting up? How could children with facial disfigurements be integrated into primary schools? What were the worries of children in care? The rights of the child were not academic; their needs had to be translated directly into action: the right to a safe environment prompted grants to improve playground safety, the right to a pain-free existence produced *Children and Pain*, a highly influential leaflet for health-care workers written by Priscilla Alderson and produced by the charity Action for Sick Children in 1992. In 1994, a training pack for magistrates and health- and child-care professionals was produced with Foundation help: *The Welfare of the Child: Assessing evidence in children cases*.

In the summer of 1993 the Foundation published *One Scandal Too Many* by Peter Newell. This report, again backed by a working group, had looked at how young people could be protected from physical and mental violence in whatever setting they found themselves. The report gave momentum to the debate about the smacking of children, something that the Gulbenkian had already been concerned with when, in 1989, it supported the establishment of a new charity called APPROACH – the Association for the Protection of All Children.

One Scandal Too Many was published not long before the James Bulger tragedy, when children were indicted in the press as scapegoats for a more general increase in violence. The Foundation was worried that its work was threatened by what it called 'the ill-informed nature of the current public debate'. Presciently it had argued: 'In Britain, the debate has been largely in the media, and has rarely been well-informed. There has been little serious examination of the substantial research findings on the causes of the development of violent attitudes and actions by children and young people.' Although other countries had looked at the totality of violence in society – whether child abuse, domestic violence, sport violence or violent crime – no such study had been undertaken in the UK, so in 1994 the Foundation decided to establish a Commission on Children and Violence, chaired by Sir William Utting, former Chief Inspector of the Social Services Inspectorate. The Utting Commission was charged with providing an accurate picture of the level of violence to and by young people and proposing ways of breaking cycles of violence. It was the first major social welfare enquiry that the Foundation had funded for a decade, and was to prove highly effective in raising levels of concern, and prompting action to combat violence involving children. But it was also controversial. Twenty of the report's 300 pages dealt with smacking, suggesting a ban, propelling the issue on to the front pages of the *Daily Mail* and the *Daily Express*, making smacking the main item on BBC news, and causing the unfortunate Utting to receive calls at home from distressed so-called 'family campaigners'.

'Before you come in Mum, I'd like you to bear the findings of the Gulbenkian Commission in mind.' Cartoon by Karl Dixon.

The Foundation was interested in helping wherever children found themselves in difficult situations, and it was adept at spotting instances that lay outside the public gaze. One of these was the plight of young carers who were looking after seriously ill or disabled parents: 'Such children . . . have surrendered their childhood; often too tired to cope at school, too embarrassed to invite a friend home.' Their numbers were estimated to be in the thousands, and the Foundation gave a grant for a pilot project to look at how other countries managed this issue, and to set up a 'befrienders' scheme.

A Foundation publication describing the experiences of young carers, 2000. Photo: Gillian Allard.

One of the Foundation's most successful initiatives in this area was the attention it paid to children in care, whose educational needs were consistently neglected. The issue was brought to the attention of Simon Richey when he read an article in the *Times Educational Supplement* based on moving personal experience. The story thereafter provides a typical example of how the Foundation works. Having uncovered a neglected field, they sought a partner, and found the right one in The Who Cares? Trust. This charity was established in 1992 to help lonely children and teenagers in care by Victoria Laughland, described by Ben Whitaker as 'a passionate pioneer . . . illuminating the voluntary world.' She died in 1994, but The Who Cares? Trust continues to do valuable work with children in care. The collaboration between the Gulbenkian and The Who Cares? Trust stimulated a government scheme to improve education and welfare for children in care. Concern for children in care continues to this day, with a recent Gulbenkian-funded project, By Degrees, dedicated to helping such children get a University education.

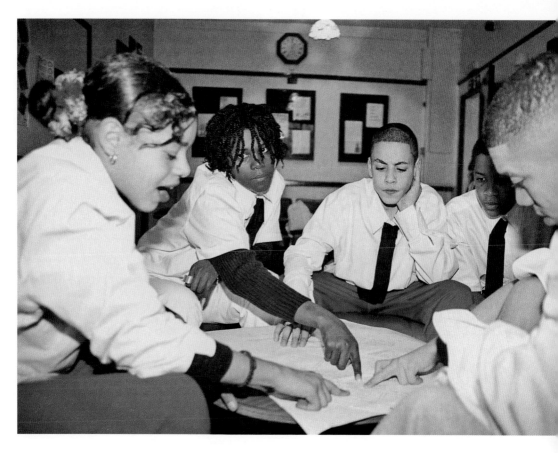

Young people in care take part in an educational project organised by The Who Cares? Trust in 2003. Photo: © Lizzy Sutcliffe.

Education: Moving Culture

The Education Reform Act was passed in 1988, at the same time as Ben Whitaker took over as the United Kingdom Branch's Director. Continuing Kim Taylor's philosophy, he oriented the Foundation's Education priorities as a counterpoint to, or compensation for, official policies. Henceforth the Gulbenkian would concentrate on 'the development of educational alternatives within the maintained sector'. An early example is a grant given in 1988 to Community Service Volunteers to investigate the possibility of a GCSE in active citizenship. This continued to be a Foundation interest and in 1992 it funded Citizenship Youth Awards in Northern Ireland.

Another Foundation concern, and one that complemented the work of the Utting Commission on Children and Violence, was bullying in schools. Until taken up by the Gulbenkian, bullying was not considered to be a major problem. In fact it might be considered a text-book example of how a foundation can identify an issue that is generally overlooked in society,

In 2003–05 the Foundation supported the Soil Association's campaign for healthier school meals and the work of Jeanette Orrey, their School Meals Policy Adviser. Pupils at St Peter's School, East Bridgeford, a Soil Association Food for Life School. Photo: Soil Association.

The Foundation's 'bullying pack', sent to every school in the UK in 1992.

stimulate interest in it, and gather together a constituency to do something about it by pushing government, public services and the voluntary sector to take the issue seriously and to act. (A similar recent example from 2005 is the scandal of school meals, highlighted by the celebrity chef Jamie Oliver, where the Foundation helped the Soil Association at a crucial moment with a grant to publish an information pack.) Bullying became a major strand of the Foundation's work, and one of its great successes: working with the television personality Esther Rantzen, the Foundation generated massive media interest, which helped bullying become a serious political issue. In 1992, the Gulbenkian sent 'bullying packs' to every school in the country, and in due course OFSTED required all schools to have an anti-bullying strategy.

Two other priorities in the early 1990s were 'parent-school relationships' and 'disaffected pupils'. A seminal work on parenting, *Confident Parents, Confident Children*, by Gillian Pugh, Erica De'Ath and Celia Smith, was reprinted by the National Children's Bureau in 1994 with a grant from the Foundation. In the mid-1990s 'education for parenthood' became an important issue, with innovatory grants, for example to Working with Men, a scheme to promote the skills and responsibilities of fatherhood, and to the Family Covenant Association, set up by Lord Young of Dartington in 1994 to

The Foundation has offered support to parents and their children in a variety of circumstances. Reproduced from the *Parenting Forum Newsletter* in 1996. Photo: Anita J. Mckenzie/Mckenzie Heritage Pictures.

Susannah York, Gemma Jones, Diana Rigg, Tim Piggott-Smith and Patricia Hodge at the launch in 1996 of the Foundation's report on discretionary awards for dance and drama students undertaken by the National Foundation for Educational Research. Photo: Morris Carpenter/Insight.

make possible a non-religious equivalent of baptism – one of several projects by Michael Young that the Foundation financed.

The arts strand of the Education Programme was influenced by the Foundation's enquiry into young people's cultural activities, published as *Moving Culture* in 1990. The report, which celebrated young people's capacity to create their own cultural forms, generated mixed reactions. Some thought that it would be a mistake for trusts and agencies to become involved in popular culture, partly because it was flourishing anyway, partly because it would occasion unwanted institutional interference where funding, if undertaken at all, needed to be subtle and hands-off. What the report achieved, however, was a loosening and relaxation of attitudes at a time when official bodies in particular were struggling to find a coherent approach. As Richey put it to us, 'The door was opened a bit wider,' enabling arts funders and out-of-school organisations to encourage such things as video and film-making, and, for example, making it possible for the rock group Iron Maiden to work with young musicians.

One of the most successful Gulbenkian interventions in arts education concerned dance and drama funding for students. Taking the initiative (although somewhat warily in financial terms), the Foundation co-funded a nationwide enquiry by the National Foundation for Education Research that discovered a horrifying patchwork: whether or not students could get a

Discover, the
Children's Discovery
Centre in East London,
presents *Space to
Imagine* in 2001.
Photo: Tzon-wei
Huang.

grant to study dance and drama was a lottery, depending on the attitude of the local authority in the area where they lived. The report – *Discretionary Awards in Dance and Drama* (1996) – was given a media-friendly launch at the Institute of Contemporary Arts by the actor Diana Rigg, accompanied by many other actors and dancers. The shadow Minister for Culture, Chris Smith, endorsed the report and the government moved swiftly to reform the system. This was a case where the Foundation's ambitious intention – to change government policy – paid off dramatically and swiftly.

Paul Curno's visits to the United States had many beneficial results for the Foundation. After visiting the Boston Children's Museum he wanted to investigate the scope for similar children's centres in the UK, and commissioned John Pearce to write *Centres for Curiosity and Imagination*, published in 1998. The result has been the creation of a network of 800 members under the auspices of the Kids' Club Network. The Foundation also went on to establish Discover (the Children's Discovery Centre), an interactive place for children and their families in Stratford, East London.

Another Country

Throughout the 1980s the Foundation had taken a great interest in inner cities. In the early 1990s attention turned to rural areas. Rural poverty was another of those unseen issues that the Foundation identified and, as it announced in 1993, decided to do something about: 'Rural poverty is all the more insidious and intractable because it often seems invisible to the public, the press, Westminster and Whitehall – whose members may carry a romanticised view of country life from holidays or weekends.' In fact, in the early 1990s the picture was grim and deteriorating, as in many ways it continues to be: low incomes, lack of transport, limited access to health services and the accelerating disappearance of shops and post offices meant that thousands of people experienced hardship. Of the officially designated 11 million rural population, 25 per cent lived on or below the poverty line. The Foundation directed its resources to tackling the issues from a variety of angles, for example funding the publication of James Derounian's *Another Country: Real life beyond rose cottage* in 1993 as well as the Action with Communities in Rural England (ACRE) report *Rural Action: A collection of community work case*

North Devon Project, a community media enterprise in a rural area, 1972.

studies. In that year forty-three of the 300 grants given were concerned with rural life in one form or another – from looking at the promotion of green tourism, to studying the viability of village shops, to the production of a video about a group of agricultural hamlets in Derbyshire.

The neglect of the countryside in terms of the arts also became a Foundation concern. In 1990 Fiona Ellis succeeded Iain Reid as Assistant Director, Arts, the first woman to be responsible for a Department since the departure of Betty Hyams in 1974, and in Ben Whitaker's opinion an appointment 'long overdue'. Born in Northern Ireland, Ellis was unusual in never having had direct contact with the Foundation before. Her professional experience was in what she described to us as 'arts with a mission', and her previous job had been as Theatre Officer with Southern Arts. Arriving some months after Reid left, she found a pile of applications, but no induction procedure or training, so she had to learn through mistakes. She told us: 'There was a Gulbenkian style, but not a Gulbenkian diktat about what you did. You had total freedom, and Mikhael Essayan was the best Trustee I have ever worked with. Putting up proposals to him was a bit like being a very junior barrister in front of a very senior judge. You had to know your brief, but he would help you through it.' She also found that in spite of Whitaker's efforts, the three Departments still operated independently of each other.

In line with the rhythm of change set for the Departments by Whitaker, the specific theme of 'Ethnic Minority Arts' modulated in 1991 into 'Cultural Equity', a programme exercising 'blatant discrimination, seeking out new applications from "minority" groups – people from racial groups, women and disabled people,' and giving particular help to women's arts organisations. Similarly 'Training for Experienced Artists' and 'Contact with Foreign Influences' were recast as 'Regeneration and Development' before being replaced in 1993 by the general heading of 'Foundation Initiatives', which included considerable investment in puppetry. This marginalised art form was to be the subject of a Foundation enquiry, followed by a report, *On the Brink of Belonging*, in 1992, and received a significant boost through help to the Puppet Centre Trust. Ellis felt her work on small-scale touring opera, for which she commissioned Graham Devlin's report *Beggars' Opera*, also published in 1992, was a good example of using Foundation resources to bring a group of practitioners together, help them set up their own

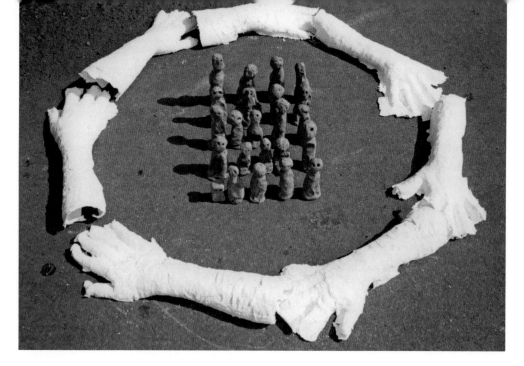

Circle of Friends: the Warley Leisure Project, inspired here by the work of sculptor Antony Gormley, assists in the provision of creative arts opportunities for people with learning disabilities.
Photo: G. Collett.

organisation, Beggars' Forum, and secure recognition for their work from the Association of British Orchestras. In her first year Ellis oversaw the final stages of the Foundation's Public Art programme, and took over a new theme that was just coming to the grant-giving stage.

Although conditions in the countryside were already a concern of the Social Welfare and Education Departments, as we have seen, this was the first time the Arts Department had become involved specifically with 'Rural Art'. The way Ellis set about tackling the generally unrecognised cultural problems created by the combination of creeping suburbanisation and widespread deprivation, which added up to an almost complete misunderstanding of rural life as a whole, compounded by a lack of arts provision, is exemplary of the approach the Foundation has developed, and amounts to a case study in its own right. The process followed a classic Foundation pattern: the scheme took two years to research and prepare, grants were made for five years, leaving recipients with a dowry to give time for other agencies to move into the field.

The decision to tackle the issue of rural art reflected long-held Foundation principles: the recognition that London and the South-East were relatively over-privileged goes back to the Bridges Report; the emphasis on community self-help and community art goes back to the late 1960s and the 1970s. Having decided to investigate the issue, in 1989 the Foundation commissioned two experienced community arts workers, Trevor Bailey and Ian Scott, to produce a discussion document, *Rural Arts*, which confirmed that there was indeed a problem that official policy, which saw the countryside only in terms of agriculture or tourism, was not addressing. The report identified needs, gave some examples of good practice, recommended that ACRE (Action with Communities in Rural England), the body linking the

Dancing Scarecrows, 1994, an arts project in Suffolk created by Moss Fuller.
Photo: © Moss Fuller.

Rural Community Councils, would be a useful partner, and set out a range of options for action.

These options were considered by an advisory panel of experts set up by the Foundation, the Rural Arts Consultation Group, which recommended that rural arts projects should be locally devised and controlled, and funded by local agencies that the Foundation would identify. These were most often local arts organisations, funded either by local authorities or Regional Arts Associations. It was the first time that the Foundation had devolved grant-making decisions to others, but this made sense, for the actual grants to be distributed were usually £100 or less. The chosen agency, say Suffolk ACRE, or the Taigh Chearsabhagh Trust in the Outer Hebrides, would be awarded £5,000 for a year's worth of grants, of which £1,000 covered their administrative costs. (If that sounds generous, the 20 per cent it represents was found to be insufficient in view of the time and travelling involved.) In March 1990 the Foundation funded a conference in Durham on the arts in rural areas, 'Pride of Place', and launched its Rural Arts Agency Scheme in midsummer with a leaflet, *Making a Song and Dance About It*.

Through the process of consultation, the Gulbenkian was able to be clear about its objectives: 'Creative content should be central.' Although community development might be a useful by-product, this was not the intention, which was to recover the lost creativity of the countryside, using both traditional forms, including crafts, and, where appropriate, new technologies such as video and broadcasting. As Fiona Ellis wrote at the time:

> We intended to help small rural communities regain their sense of pride and
> also a sense of community cohesiveness. The arts would be the tool by which
> people who had perhaps not worked together before came together as a team
> and learned team-building skills . . . We also put a considerable emphasis on
> obtaining as high quality an outcome as possible.

The scheme inevitably had to engage with the vexed relationship between 'professional' and 'amateur' artists, and although about half the projects did use professional artists in some way (and appreciated their work) Ellis appears to have learned some of the lessons of the Foundation's involvement in community art: 'It is an important factor that the projects are "owned" and controlled by the participants and not by professional community artists who sometimes parachute into a village full of good intentions and then leave everyone flat when they go off to the next challenge.'

The scheme, re-titled 'A Sense of Place' in 1991, ran until the beginning of 1996. Some 200 individual projects had been funded by then, and twenty-five agencies involved. The final grants made were to last three years, so by December 1985 the cost of the scheme to the Foundation came to £550,000. The actual projects ranged from the revival of the Great Torrington Furze Dance, to the creation of an oral history of a Royal Air Force base at Swanton Morley, to the Swimbridge Church Kneeler Project in Devon. But the Foundation was not content simply to see its money spent. In 1995 it commissioned Dr Tess Hurson, an expert on rural arts, to carry out an evaluation, which it published, warts and all, in 1996 as *Did We Do That?* As Fiona Ellis put it, it was important 'to warn future grant-makers of pitfalls into which we have stumbled'. Hurson's report discusses the failures as well as the successes of the scheme, and the lessons to be learned. It is evident that the aesthetic issues were complex, for 'high art', urban aesthetic values are so dominant that 'it is hardly surprising that agents are at times in some difficulty as to how to measure the aesthetic benefits of the scheme.'

The real problem that Hurson's evaluation throws up, however, is that of the Foundation's inability to act as a long-term funder. Hurson pronounced the scheme a success, but the Foundation's involvement was finite. Rural arts agencies had developed useful practices and partnerships, but it needed someone else to carry the scheme on. There was hope that ACRE would be able to use the models that had been created to argue for more resources from its funder, the then Rural Development Commission (which merged with the Countryside Commission to form the Countryside Agency in 1999). The scheme petered out after 1999, although some projects were able to

Did We Do That?
The Foundation's evaluation in 1996 of its Rural Arts Agency Scheme.
Photo: Piers Rawson.

183

find funding through the National Lottery. The Foundation did, however, fund ACRE to produce *A Rural Arts Handbook*, published in 1997. The Gulbenkian thus completed the cycle of this exemplary project with a legacy of knowledge and skills that has long-term use.

Science and Art

In October 1995 Fiona Ellis left the Foundation to widen her experience of grant-making beyond the field of the arts, and in 1997 became Director of the Northern Rock Foundation, based in Newcastle. She was succeeded as Arts Director by Siân Ede who had been a drama officer at the Arts Council for sixteen years, latterly combining that with teaching arts and education management part time at City University. While at the Arts Council she had secured support from the Foundation and the Esmée Fairbairn Foundation for a strengthening of the theatre directors' training scheme that had been created in the wake of the Foundation's 1989 report, *A Better Direction*.

Ede's arrival coincided with a change-point in the Branch's policy cycle, as first the Rural Arts and then the Cultural Equity programmes were phased out. The new themes that were developed represented in some senses a return to the Foundation's traditions. The 'community' aspect was represented by a programme aimed exclusively at the amateur sector (even excluding the amateur-involving outreach schemes of professional organisations) to stimulate 'Participatory Music', a new term coined by the Foundation to describe non-professional music-making in all its forms, as surveyed by Anthony Everitt in his 1997 report for the Gulbenkian report, *Joining In*. The Foundation's commitment to individual artists, and their need for time for research and development, as opposed to performance, was renewed by two schemes, launched in 1996, 'Time to Experiment', and 'Creative Use of New Technologies'. Fiona Ellis's interest in computers – she persuaded the Foundation to buy her a laptop – had led her to commission Owen Kelly's report, *Digital Creativity*, published in 1996. Out of the interest in technology grew a programme that found a way to address the neglected, indeed long-abandoned, fourth category in the Gulbenkian's founding statutes, Science.

The idea to explore the possibilities of creating new connections between science and art was very much Siân Ede's own. She had been struck by the increase in popular interest in science during the 1980s, stimulated by the success of books like Stephen Hawkings's *A Brief History of Time*, and by the fact that scientists were aware of a greater need to explain themselves: 'Scientists were using phrases we thought belonged to us: the "meaning" of life; "the nature of the self" ... And also words that artists had rejected: "beauty" and "elegance".' At the same time there was a *need* for scientists to explain themselves, as their work, from genetic codes to outer space, raised ever more complex issues of humanity and ethics.

The first step, in 1994, was to commission The Arts Catalyst, an independent agency founded (with a start-up grant from the Foundation) in 1993 to broker links between artists and scientists, to explore the possibilities of a programme to produce science-inspired art works. The results encouraged the Foundation to absorb its new technology strand into 'Two Cultures – The Arts and Science', announced in the 1996 *Annual Report* with the hope that 'the astonishing implications of genetic research, quantum physics, space exploration, chaos theory, number theory and so on must

Participatory Music. A multicultural music project, *The Bridge*, organised by South Wales Intercultural Community Arts. Photo: Terry Morgan.

Ackroyd & Harvey, *Blasted Oak*, 1999. A dead oak tree covered with grass grown from seed. From *Secret Gardens*, Wilton House Wiltshire. Commissioned by Salisbury Arts Festival. Courtesy of the artists.

surely affect artistic creativity.' To ensure that they did, in the following years the Foundation channelled funds through The Arts Catalyst, The Laboratory at the Ruskin School of Drawing and Fine Art at Oxford, the Institute of Contemporary Arts, ArtsLab at Imperial College London and the Interalia Centre in Bristol. Arts Catalyst, for instance, arranged a residency at Imperial College for the American sculptor James Acord, whose interest in radioactive materials (beginning with sculptor's granite) had led him to become the only artist in the world licensed to handle nuclear material. Here was a genuine case of the philosopher's stone, as Acord transmuted the dross of fissile waste into memorial-like reliquaries.

Acord was doing precisely what Siân Ede had hoped. She argued:

Artists, like the rest of us, must learn the new language necessary for an understanding of science, engaging even in highly technical methodologies. For if we do not begin to understand the culture, we will not be respected for our grasp of the issues involved and will lay ourselves open to being ignorant or sentimental or trivial, able at best to make playful but unhelpful distortions.

The quotation is from *Strange and Charmed: Science and the contemporary visual arts*, published by the Gulbenkian in 2000. Edited by Siân Ede, and with substantial contributions by her alongside those from artist and scientist collaborators, the book is representative of the more ambitious publishing that the United Kingdom Branch has undertaken since 1998.

'Scientists must be persuaded to view their work, at every stage, from the perspective of others,' wrote Ede, making the point that the science–art relationship should not be a one-way street. Individual scientists have subsequently become willing to collaborate with artists in the interests of

Kitsou Dubois, *Gravity Zero*, 1999. The choreographer worked with astronauts to assist them in combating motion sickness in zero gravity. In a project facilitated by The Arts Catalyst she joined the Biodynamics Group at Imperial College London, to research physiological responses to movement in space. The video of her parabolic flights is shown as an artwork in its own right. Courtesy of the artist, Ki Productions and The Arts Catalyst.

extending their science, but, as the highly computer-literate artist Neal White discovered when he held a residency (residencies being no longer the anomalies they had been in the 1960s) at the Human Genome Mapping Project near Cambridge, scientists could learn the language of art. Michael Rhodes, a scientist on the Genome Mapping Project, commented: 'I now understand what the artist is trying to do. The amazing revelation for me is that art should not be explained . . . A scientist explains: an artist provokes a response.'

The programme worked best when artists and scientists were able to collaborate, without compromising their individual disciplines. A case in point is the Quaking Houses Wetlands Project, a remarkable scheme in that it synthesises not only science and art but other important Foundation themes: community enterprise and responsibility, education and environ-mentalism, and public art. Quaking Houses is a Durham pit village virtually abandoned by the economic imperatives of the 1980s, and facing a major environmental hazard from its derelict mine workings. The scientific solution was to create a wetland that would deal with the poisonous pollution ecologically and form a nature reserve, but the Sunderland-based Artists' Agency (since renamed Helix Arts), with whom the Foundation had worked on public art schemes in the 1980s, also became involved. In 1998, with new funds from the Gulbenkian, the Artists' Agency commissioned the artist Helen Smith to design the physical setting for the process in order to create safe public access, while local people, working through their own Quaking Houses Environmental Trust, helped to create it. A craftworker, Lee Dalby, was also commissioned to make willow-sculptures enhancing the site. The project could not solve all the social issues of educational deprivation, unemployment and disaffection faced by Quaking Houses, but art and science were both at the service of the community.

The Arts and Science programme ended in 2002, but by then not only had the scheme had a significant impact, both on individual artists and on creating the climate for the success of many other endeavours, but new alliances had also been formed, and new sources of funding found. One reason for stopping, Siân Ede told us, was that the theme 'had become mainstream'. Ede worked closely with Ken Arnold, Head of Public Programmes at Britain's largest and richest charity, the Wellcome Trust – dedicated to biomedical research – which had initiated the Sciart scheme

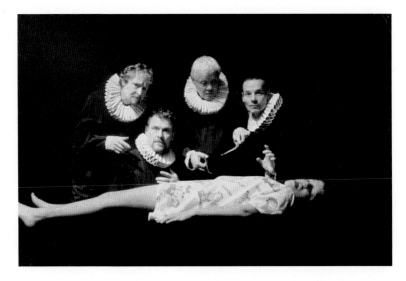

A still from *Mapping Perception*, 2002, a film and accompanying installation by artist/film-maker Andrew Kötting in collaboration with neuroscientist Mark Lythgoe, looking at the world through the perceptions of Eden Kötting, who has a rare genetic disorder, Joubert's Syndrome.

in 1996. The Gulbenkian's Arts and Science programme was a mirror image of the Wellcome's, encouraging artists to engage with science for art's sake, rather than as a means of facilitating the public's engagement with science. When the Wellcome Board questioned the value of Sciart the Gulbenkian joined a consortium of other funders, Arts Council England, the British Council, the Scottish Arts Council and NESTA, to maintain the Wellcome Sciart scheme for a further three years. This proved so successful that the Wellcome Board expanded its involvement with art as part of a broader and more confident programme of public engagement. The Foundation meanwhile continues to work with other agencies such as the Royal Society, the Royal Society of Medicine, the Natural History Museum and the Science Museum.

1999: the Social Impact of the Arts

When Ben Whitaker retired as Director of the United Kingdom Branch, both Britain and the Gulbenkian Foundation were again on the cusp of change. In 1993 Dr Perdigão died in office, shortly before his ninety-seventh birthday, having led the Foundation as Chairman of the Trustees since 1956. His successor, Professor António Ferrer Correia, served as Chairman until 1998; on his retirement, his place was taken by Dr Victor de Sá Machado, who in his inaugural speech as Chairman stressed the need for modernisation throughout the Foundation. The Foundation's commitment to the United Kingdom Branch remained. Indeed, during Whitaker's directorship the Branch's annual distribution of grants had risen from just under £1.5 million in 1989 to £2 million in 1999.

In a mood of pre-millennial tension, Britain waited to see what the New Labour government, elected in 1997, would do to address the problems of social and educational deprivation that had built up since the Conservatives had taken office in 1979. The economy was recovering from the recession of the early 1990s, but society was much more divided than it had been, and a new term 'the underclass' had come into use. In 1979 there were, officially, 5 million poor; in 1989 there were 12 million. The poorest got poorer, and the rich much richer, but the latter showed little inclination, in Whitaker's opinion, to share their wealth even by starting new foundations. The new government promised to address pressing social issues, in particular through investment in health services and education, but their commitment to observing the previous Conservative spending plans for two years meant that it was not until the new financial year began in 1999 that new money, as opposed to new rhetoric, was forthcoming.

Similar spending constraints affected public spending on the arts, where budgets had effectively been frozen since 1992. But the funding landscape, both for the arts and charities, had been significantly changed by the decision of John Major's government in 1992 to launch a National Lottery. Major also decided that Britain should at last have a cultural ministry, with a Secretary of State of Cabinet rank. In 1997 this, the Department of National Heritage, was renamed by Labour the Department for Culture, Media and Sport. The Gulbenkian's United Kingdom Branch, representing as it did the 'good causes' of both the arts and charities, responded quickly on behalf of the voluntary sector to the government's 1992 Lottery White Paper. In order to help them understand the implications of this new phenomenon, Whitaker commissioned as one of his first reports, *Good Cause for Gambling? The prospects for a National Lottery in the UK* by John Kay, a consultant and Professor at the London Business School. There were fears that a National Lottery would allow governments to shrug off various direct responsibilities by diverting funds to their own conceptions of social priorities (fears which, in spite of politicians' protestations, have become reality), and that charities would suffer financially because of a decline in charitable giving, and competition for their own, already licensed, local lotteries. Kay warned that 'charities are likely to lose income', but set against that the prospect of their receiving at least £325 million a year from the National Lottery Charities Board, one of the five original good causes (along with arts, heritage, sport and the Millennium Commission). Kay's report came down in favour of the National Lottery, which 'should be implemented, as soon as feasible.' Four good causes came on stream in 1994, but Home Office dilatoriness meant that the charities had to wait until 1995.

The Arts Department was in a different position, since at first arts Lottery money was only to go to capital projects, which it was not Foundation policy to fund. It was also the case that every Lottery applicant had to find a percentage of funding from elsewhere, but again, the Foundation made it a policy not to give matching grants. This was an extension of Whitaker's principle of not giving money to replace sums cut by the government 'lest', as he wrote in 1995, 'doing so might only encourage the Treasury to cut further.' Under pressure from criticism of the perceived élitism of early capital grants, such as to the Royal Opera House, and the fear of having brand-new buildings with nothing going on in them, Lottery rules were gradually relaxed, beginning with the Arts for Everyone scheme in 1997, which took over projects similar to those that the Foundation had funded through its Rural Arts programme. Between 1996 and 1998 the United Kingdom Branch experienced a fall in the overall number of applications, but it was not clear if the Lottery was the reason. On the whole the effect of the National Lottery on the Foundation was benign. As Siân Ede told us: 'Our principle was that we didn't do matching funding – we like to start things, not simply top them off. But the Lottery made things feel buoyant. The capital projects meant that there were good spaces to be in, such as the refurbishment of The Place dance centre, where we could fund experimental activities.' On the other hand, although it is difficult to prove a connection, charitable giving fell in Britain between 1993 and 1998 by 31 per cent.

In 1998 the Labour government introduced a revising National Lottery Act, which sanctioned the use of Lottery money for revenue funding, and introduced a requirement that Lottery distributors should be more 'strategic' in their grant-giving. It also created a sixth 'good cause', the New Opportunities Fund, thus reducing the portions of the other five, and giving the government an opportunity to fund its own projects in the fields of health, education and the environment. It also established the National Endowment for Science, Technology and the Arts (NESTA). Since then the government has continued to encroach on the funding streams of the original Lottery distributors, and has wound up the Millennium Commission. The government-controlled Big Lottery Fund now absorbs half of all the income derived from the National Lottery.

In spite of being used to co-operating with public funders such as the Arts Council, the United Kingdom Branch found that it was working in a changed administrative climate. The so-called New Public Management developed in the 1980s had imposed the principles of Value for Money and performance indicators throughout the public sphere, and the use of service agreements between government departments and those it funded had created a 'contract culture' where organisations had to demonstrate their efficiency in meeting targets and climbing league tables. It might be argued that the Foundation had contributed to this highly instrumental approach by funding the Myerscough Report, *The Economic Importance of the Arts in Britain*, in 1988. This had helped to spread the language of 'the cultural industries'; as Labour's first Arts Minister, Mark Fisher, said at the launch of New Labour's cultural policy document *Create the Future* before the election in 1997, 'Culture creates jobs.' Yet the excessively instrumental and econo-mistic approach to the arts was being questioned, and once again it was the Foundation that helped to change the terms of the debate.

In 1995 the United Kingdom Branch agreed to help fund a study of the social, as opposed to economic, impact of the arts by the independent research group, Comedia. Founded by Charles Landry in 1978, Comedia had already undertaken research reports for the Foundation: *Out of Hours*, a study of leisure activity in cities published in 1991, and a study of urban parks, *Park Life*, published in 1995. In 1993 it had carried out a short study for the Arts Council on the social impact of the arts, and it now wished to develop a major research project. As the United Kingdom Branch's internal assessment of the application said: 'The study, *The Social Impact of the Arts*, aims to do what *The Economic Impact of the Arts* omitted: i.e. to make the case for the social value of arts work without which the economic argument is barren.' A grant of £7,500 was made towards an anticipated cost of £40,000, which proved useful in attracting further funds.

The final report, written by François Matarasso and titled *Use or Ornament? The social impact of participation in the arts,* appeared in 1997, shortly after Labour had taken office. It was to go into several editions. It was the largest social study of the arts in Britain ever undertaken, and it also had an international dimension. It took as its subject the 'participatory arts', recognising the social and cultural value of the community arts (promoted by the Gulbenkian since the late 1960s, as we have seen). The emphasis was not on evaluating qualitative change in the arts themselves, but changes produced by their impact on social behaviours and well-being, using social research methodologies rather than those deployed by economists. It argued that 'social impacts are demonstrable', and that it was possible to arrive at workable indicators. The report listed no fewer than fifty different social outcomes, from No. 1: 'Increase people's confidence and sense of self-worth' to No. 50: 'Provide a unique and deep source of enjoyment'.

Quite how quantifiable or measurable these benefits were has since been challenged, but *Use or Ornament?* changed the terms of the debate and provided a new argument for funding the arts. In practice, economic evaluation of projects did not disappear, and the importance of the social impact of the arts began to be applied as instrumentally as the economic ones, but at least the argument was not as crudely utilitarian as the economic arguments of the 1980s. Once again, the Gulbenkian Foundation, as a co-funder of the report, was helping to set the agenda. As Matarasso wrote in his foreword:

> The election of a Government committed to tackling problems like youth unemployment, fear of crime and social exclusion is the right moment to start talking about what the arts can do for society, rather than what society can do for the arts. Unfettered by ideology, the new pragmatism can extend its principle of inclusiveness to the arts by embracing their creative approaches to problem-solving. Britain deserves better than the exhausted prejudices of post-war debates over state support for the arts.

Having played an important part in those debates, the United Kingdom Branch of the Gulbenkian Foundation could only agree.

CHAPTER 5

Into the twenty-first century

'We remain on the lookout for the quirky and the innovative . . . we hope that the truly amazing will not be overlooked.'

PAULA RIDLEY, *ANNUAL REPORT* 2003

The opening of a new century has seen the United Kingdom Branch both reformed and reinvigorated. A new Director has introduced important changes while maintaining the creative spirit of the organisation. In this final chapter we describe the effects of renewed government involvement in social policy that has affected the scope for independent action. A significant feature of recent years has been the successful development of a Programme of Anglo-Portuguese Cultural Relations. The chapter concludes with an account of the distinctive qualities that have sustained the achievements of the United Kingdom Branch of the Gulbenkian Foundation over the past half-century.

OPPOSITE: The inaugural award of the Gulbenkian Prize for Museums and Galleries, May 2003, was won by the National Centre for Citizenship and the Law at the Galleries of Justice in Nottingham. Left to right: Michiel Stevenson and Peter Armstrong, Chairman and Chief Executive of the Galleries of Justice; Dr Emílio Rui Vilar, Chairman of the Calouste Gulbenkian Foundation; Bamber Gascoigne, Chairman of the Judges; Baroness Blackstone, Minister for the Arts; and Tim Desmond, Head of Education, Galleries of Justice. Photo: Joe Miles.

26 May 2005

We are back in Portland Place, but this time a hundred yards down the street, at the Royal Institute of British Architects. Three hundred guests are waiting in the 1930s grandeur of the Florence Hall for the announcement of the winner of the biggest art prize in Britain, the £100,000 Gulbenkian Prize for Museums and Galleries. The United Kingdom Branch Director, Paula Ridley, is talking to Lady Cobham, Chairman of the Museum Prize, the charity that administers the award. Mikhael Essayan is also present, keeping his customary low profile, but also here is another Gulbenkian Board member, Dr Teresa Gouveia, who has come from Lisbon for the occasion, and who will affirm the Foundation's pride in 'our independence and our capacity for developing adventurous new ideas' during the awards ceremony. Sixty museums, from very great to very small, have entered the

The winner of the 2004 Gulbenkian Prize was the Scottish National Gallery of Modern Art, Edinburgh, for *Landform*, by Charles Jencks. Photo: Alistair Linford.

Paula Ridley, Director of the UK Branch, greets HRH The Prince of Wales at the 1999 Gulbenkian Awards for British Museums and Galleries, held at the National Gallery in London, and organised by the Museums Association. In the background are Neil MacGregor, then Director of the National Gallery (left), and Mark Taylor, Director of the Museums Association. Photo: Museums Association.

competition and four are on the short list. The judges, among them Sir Neil Chalmers, former Director of the Natural History Museum, and the broadcaster Joan Bakewell, are chaired by the Rector of Imperial College London, Sir Richard Sykes.

At the start of the speeches David Lammy, who has just become the new Minister for Culture in the Department for Culture, Media and Sport, says a few friendly words about 'a revival in the museums sector' and there is a rumble of approval in the hall when he talks of growth and mentions the Heritage Lottery Fund, which has grant-aided all four museums on the short list. There are cheers when the winner is announced: Big Pit, the National Mining Museum of Wales at Blaenafon, which opened in 1983 and is still staffed by miners who lost their jobs when the pit closed. A gruff Welsh voice thanks the judges – and promises 'to milk the prize for all it's worth'.

The Gulbenkian Prize is a rare example of the United Kingdom Branch returning to an earlier scheme. In 1989 Ben Whitaker, convinced that in the UK museums were a neglected area, decided to raise the visibility of British museums 'and try to make them more welcoming'. He decided to support the Museum of the Year awards scheme, established by the charity National Heritage in 1973, by giving the Museums Association £15,000 over three years to create prizes for user-friendliness, including improved catering. Later, he set up a similar, cross-border museums award scheme in Ireland. The Foundation continued to fund these Gulbenkian Awards until 1999, when it was decided that they needed rethinking. In 2000 a £20,000 re-launch grant helped set up the new Museum Prize charity, in the hope that it would be able to raise its funds from elsewhere to run the awards. But it wasn't until 2002, when Ridley decided that it was time to make a big gesture, and guarantee a £100,000 prize for five years, that there was progress. The size of the prize was a huge step-change from the £10,000 grants made in Whitaker's time, but the Board in Lisbon was persuaded, and the first Gulbenkian Prize for Museums and Galleries was awarded in 2003.

This is only one of the many changes that Ridley has introduced since becoming the first woman to be appointed Director of the United Kingdom Branch, in October 1999. Like many staff members before, she had previous experience of the Foundation. A Liverpudlian by adoption, in the 1980s she had been employed by the Centre for Employment Initiatives and Director of a charity, the Community Initiatives Research Trust, set up by the CEI, and had collaborated with Richard Mills on the Foundation's 'Community Challenge' conference in Liverpool in the immediate aftermath of the Toxteth riots in 1981. She later became a director of the Merseyside Development Corporation, and until the end of 2005 was Chairman of the Liverpool Housing Action Trust. She also served as a Trustee of the Tate and the National Gallery, and in 1998 she became Chairman of the Board of Trustees of the Victoria and Albert Museum, so it is not surprising that officially her time at Portland Place is limited to three days a week.

Ridley's memories of the United Kingdom Branch in earlier days were of how grand it was: 'A hot lunch, served by a waiter in a white coat, it was quite unlike any other charity I knew.' This impression was confirmed by Siân Ede, who told us that when she joined in 1995, 'it was like a gentleman's club, very old-fashioned and male-dominated.' But by 2000 there was a need to move on. Ridley told us, 'My mission was to modernise the institution.' This meant that the live-in caretakers had to go, along with two full-time cooks. The Gulbenkian restaurant is no more, and the household staff is down to one – though Barry Chorlton will still sometimes appear wearing a white coat. More seriously, the offices were fully comput-erised, and the building modestly refurbished (in 1990 the Foundation's early fax machine had been accepted as an exhibit by the Science Museum).

Ridley wanted to put as much of the Branch's money as possible into grants, so when Paul Curno retired as the widely respected Deputy Director in July 2001, she took over the Social Welfare Programme herself, while continuing to run a Director's Grants Programme, currently £150,000 a year. In 2004 Siân Ede was promoted to Deputy Director. Reflecting on this process of change, she told us, 'The spirit of the Branch has changed – we just got modern really, but without losing the idiosyncrasy. We don't spend lots of time on strategy meetings. You can still burst into someone's office with a new idea you've just had on the bus. Things happen in a very informal way.'

The original Departments of the United Kingdom Branch continue as before with the addition of a re-invigorated Anglo-Portuguese Cultural Relations Programme. The Arts Department, currently focusing on research and development for artists, had the largest budget allocation in 2005 of £520,000. Social Welfare, with £470,000, continues to help communities to help themselves and is principally concerned with capacity building in local groups and neighbourhoods.

The Labour government of 1997 came into power reciting a mantra of 'education, education, education'. Given this level of government concern, commitment, and consequent expenditure, the Foundation had to consider its position: did it still have a role in education? The answer was first to home in on the most needy children, and second to find pockets of 'educational innovation' overlooked by the government. The Education Department, with a total budget in 2005 of £435,000, continues to give support to schools so that they can help parents whose children are at important stages in their development, and it also funds arts activities for the excluded in Pupil Referral Units and within in-school Learning Support Units. Although unglamorous, the work in Pupil Referral Units has continued for ten years: at any one time, some 9,000 young people are permanently excluded from school, and 320,000 are excluded temporarily. There is no doubt that this large number of young people find themselves at the bottom of the educational ladder, but the evidence clearly shows that those involved benefit from arts programmes.

Under the broad theme of 'Emotional Well-being' the Foundation has supported a number of initiatives, from the issue of bullying to citizenship classes, but when the Department for Education and Skills introduced Personal, Social and Health Education (PSHE) lessons into the curriculum,

Pupils from The Windsor Boys' School Learning Support Unit, which is based at the local Arts Centre, taking part in a dance project, 2004. Photo: Pauline King.

A sense of direction: the Foundation's framework for Personal, Social and Health Education in schools helped provide PSHE with coherence, continuity and progression.
Photo: Arhon Thomas.

many found the official approach lacking in rigour and incoherent. The Foundation commissioned the publication *PASSPORT*, written by Jane Lees and Sue Plant, which provides a framework for teachers to create a comprehensive and understandable course on personal and social development for pupils across the many areas covered by PSHE. *PASSPORT* was sent to all schools and has become almost an official document.

In 2002 a major schools project, called PIP – Parent Information Point – began with the National Family and Parenting Institute as partner, to provide all parents with information on child development at 'key moments'. Unusually, this service is not targeted at particular groups but is available to any parent. It was piloted in three Local Education Authority areas and proved very effective, and was also endorsed in the government green paper *Every Child Matters*. An earlier parenting publication, *Tomorrow's Parents*, was launched by Estelle Morris when Secretary of State for Education, and was sent to every school. It provided good guidance on developing education for parenthood in schools but the government failed to follow it through; parenting education is now standard practice in Youth Offending Institutions, but still not in all schools.

Throughout his tenure as Deputy Director, Social Welfare, Paul Curno had pursued a big ambition: 'to help ensure a fairer distribution of resources, services and opportunities in favour of people living in poverty, and to assist in the development of a more inclusive democracy by encouraging the flow of information between disadvantaged groups and policy-makers.' He had a particular concern for the promotion of social enterprise, for crime and justice issues, and, as we have seen, for the welfare of children. In all three cases the Foundation pursued a strategy of maximising the impact of its resources by investing sometimes quite small sums in organisations with outstanding track records. In the year of his retirement, the Foundation's support for children's rights reached something of a culmination with its publication of the *UK Review of Effective Government Structures for Children 2001*, which brought the Foundation's 1996 report up to date. Immediately prior to the publication the government announced the creation of a Children and Young People's Unit.

Some issues that the Foundation has been active in promoting for decades have, in this new century, started to flow into the mainstream of official practice. In 2002 the Department for Trade and Industry adopted community enterprise as a part of government policy and produced a major report. This was rapidly followed by the Gulbenkian's own publication *Social Enterprise in Anytown*, by John Pearce, an early advocate of community enterprise. The Foundation has always been interested in new organisational models and ways of doing things and in 2003 published the Public Management Foundation's *Public Interest: New models for delivering public services?*, as well as funding the Association of Chief Executives of Voluntary

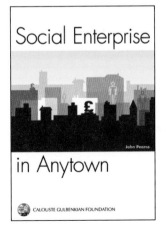
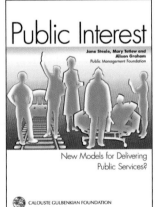
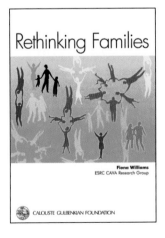

Publications from the Social Welfare Programme.

Dormanstown in Teesside lies close to the perimeter fence of a large chemical complex. Friends of the Earth helped local residents form a community group, called Impact, to tackle the environmental problems they face. Photo: Friends of the Earth Trust.

Organisations' *Replacing the State? The case for third sector public service delivery*. It was noted that the government's 'preference for the social enterprise model – long championed by the Foundation' – raised issues that echoed those of the 1980s and 1990s: once again the involvement of the third sector in the delivery of government services has 'led to excitement and unrealistic expectations on both sides'; once more the sector faced issues of capacity building. This concern has been followed through with grants explicitly aimed at increasing capacity and financial literacy, such as a grant to Hull Council for Voluntary Service to establish a network of Treasurers of not-for-profit groups.

Recent *Annual Reports* show the Foundation keeping faith with organisations that they have funded for many years – when they come up with fresh ideas. One example is a grant made in 2003 to the Runnymede Trust – which first received Foundation support in 1974 – to design and evaluate a Black History Month directory for use in schools and colleges.

The Social Welfare Programme has also moved into environmental issues and the plight of asylum seekers, while supporting schemes for the elderly. Its publication *Rethinking Families* (2004) considers the relationship patterns that are replacing those of the traditional nuclear family. It is anticipated that the environment will become an area of interest for the

Mark Fairnington, *Specimen (3)*, 2000. Oil on canvas, 92.5 x 76 cm. Private Collection. Courtesy of the artist. Fairnington's residency at Oxford University Museum of Natural History was facilitated by The Laboratory at the Ruskin School of Drawing and Fine Art.

National Student
Drama Festival:
See You Swoon by
Dartington College
2003.
Photo: © Allan
Titmuss.

Foundation. Many of the environmental projects include an element of community building, such as helping to develop sustainable food chains, while one in particular shows the Foundation's knack of addressing multiple priorities with a single grant – £10,000 to the Black Environment Network to enable them to repair and recycle bicycles for asylum seekers. Another case of synergy between Programmes is the Foundation's publication in 2004 of *Wild Reckoning*, where the arts and the environment meet in an anthology provoked by the fortieth anniversary of Rachel Carson's seminal book *Silent Spring*.

The Arts Department continues to fund contemporary dance, music, opera, theatre and art, and maintains its long-term commitment to professional training by funding the workshop programme of the National Student Drama Festival for practitioners at the very start of their careers. It is funding research into the legacy of the Artist Placement Group, which it supported in the 1970s, and, more than thirty years on from the Anderson report *Training in the Conservation of Paintings*, a grant has been made to the World Monuments Trust for training in the conservation of sculpture.

But it is the activities of a fourth Department, which we have had to put to one side till now, which have undergone the most interesting changes in recent years.

Portuguese Affairs and Anglo-Portuguese Cultural Relations

The United Kingdom Branch has, throughout its existence, acted as a home-from-home for Portuguese students on Gulbenkian bursaries, together with members of the Armenian community and, in the early days, students from the Middle East. The need to find long-term accommodation for visiting students and others led to the creation of a Student Welfare office, which in 1978 became the Portuguese Affairs Department, funded directly by Lisbon and led until 1995 by the formidable Maria Antónia da Silva. Students were visited in their universities, and an annual party at Portland Place has become a long-standing tradition. The Department not only had to see to the pastoral care of students sponsored in Britain (in 2004 there were thirty-eight on Lisbon-funded Foundation Scholarships), but also manage the many professional exchanges between London and Lisbon, and meet the needs of the Gulbenkian Orchestra and Gulbenkian Ballet Company, as well as facilitate medical visits to London by people sent by the Foundation's Health and Social Welfare Department in Lisbon.

When Kim Taylor arrived as Director he brought with him an enthusiasm for Portugal and things Portuguese, as well as a good working knowledge of the Portuguese language. Following the re-organisation of responsibilities between London and Lisbon in 1982, he launched a major new Programme, funded by the Branch, to nurture Anglo-Portuguese Cultural Relations. Two principles were clearly articulated: there would be a requirement for co-operation between the two countries and a need 'actively to create new cultural interactions'. Soon there was an opportunity to give the Programme added momentum and a fresh focus.

1986 marked the 600th anniversary of the signing of the Treaty of Windsor between Portugal and England. The treaty, which created a military and political alliance and a free trading area, is the oldest diplomatic agreement between any two countries anywhere in the world. In most of modern history Portugal and England have faced a common enemy – either France or Spain or both – depending on the ebb and flow of politics. What is more extraordinary is that the friendship has been unbroken and regularly renewed, through treaties, royal marriages, a common seafaring tradition, military co-operation and continuous trade. Cultural exchange between the two countries has deep roots as well. Three of Portugal's most eminent modern writers, Almeida Garrett, Eça de Queirós and Fernando Pessoa, all had English connections, and have been published in English translation with support from the United Kingdom Branch.

In anticipation of the celebrations of 1986 a new Anglo-Portuguese Foundation was established by the Branch in 1984, and its first task was to organise a year-long festival, *Portugal 600*. The joint patrons of the new Foundation were the Portuguese Ambassador and the Duke of Wellington, and the anniversary of the Treaty itself was celebrated in great style at Windsor Castle, with the Queen and the Prime Minister both attending.

But the Anglo-Portuguese Cultural Relations Programme was not limited to celebration of this event. Two important publishing programmes were initiated in association with Carcanet Press: 'Aspects of Portugal', covering academic studies of Portuguese history and culture, and 'From the Portuguese', a series of English translations of Portuguese poetry and fiction. Kim Taylor had a good deal of hands-on involvement, editing and designing some of the books in collaboration with Eugénio Lisboa, the Cultural Counsellor at the Portuguese Embassy in London. An Anglo-Portuguese youth

Books from the 'Aspects of Portugal' and 'From the Portuguese' series published in association with Carcanet Press.

Josefa de Óbidos,
*Still Life: Sweets and
Flowers*, 1676. Oil on
Canvas, 85 x 160.5 cm.
Collection: Santarém,
Câmara Municipal.
The first exhibition
in the UK of this
seventeenth-century
Portuguese artist was
held at the new
European Academy in
London, 1997.

exchange was begun, as was a sculpture exchange programme, and a collaboration with the BBC for a series of broadcasts entitled *Discovering Portuguese*. The common seafaring tradition of the two countries was reflected in the Branch's support for various activities within Operation Raleigh, a sailing scheme for young people. The Branch nurtured cultural relations in other ways as well, by buying paintings for Lisbon, establishing the first-ever Portuguese translation prize, organising artist exchanges, and promoting contemporary Portuguese culture through concerts and exhibitions.

In July 1999 a reorganisation took place. The Anglo-Portuguese Cultural Relations Programme, previously overseen directly by Ben Whitaker, merged on his retirement with the Portuguese Affairs Department, under a new Assistant Director, Miguel Santos, a graduate of Lisbon University and a former music journalist. He had previously worked at the Portuguese Arts Trust (the Anglo-Portuguese Foundation had changed its name twice, first to Portugal 600 in 1991, and then to the Portuguese Arts Trust) , which was now finally wound down and its functions brought 'in house'. There was consequently a 50 per cent increase in the grants budget, to £318,000, the number of grants doubled, and their scope widened. Two radical innovations followed that breathed new life into the Programme. Miguel Santos saw that in addition to funding translations and books about Portugal, the popular appreciation of Portuguese culture in the UK could be promoted by

a more contemporary route in the form of a CD. *Exploratory Music from Portugal* was sent to music venues and promoters, and distributed free with *The Wire* magazine, succeeding in introducing first-class young Portuguese musicians to a wide UK audience. The release of a CD has now become an annual event, while Miguel Santos himself has become a personal advocate for Portuguese music, hosting a weekly show on Resonance FM – the first-ever British radio programme dedicated to music of Portuguese origin.

Having produced the CD, the next step, as Santos explained to us, was to give British audiences the opportunity to see and hear the music live. So began, in 2001, the first of the annual *Atlantic Waves* festivals involving more than thirty artists. Taken together, these initiatives have put Portuguese music into the mainstream of British culture, and have helped to promote

Dulwich Picture Gallery organised an education programme with support from the Foundation in connection with Paula Rego's exhibition there in 1998.
Photo: Len Cross.

Atlantic Waves 2002.
Fado singer Mariza performs at the Purcell Room, South Bank Centre.
Photo: Alex Delfanne.

the careers of Portuguese performers. A vivid example is Mariza, a singer of traditional Fado music. Under the auspices of the Foundation she visited the UK in 2002, and her song *Primavera* appears on the 2002 CD. In 2003 she won the prestigious BBC Radio Three World Music Award and is now enjoying a global celebrity. The first steps have been taken to extend the model used in the case of music into other art forms, with a dance festival in 2004 and 2005.

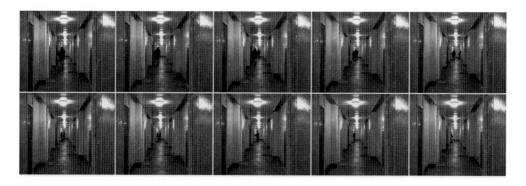

Corridor Action from Miguel Faleiro's *Rehearsing Public Quarters*, a series of three video screenings shown at the National Film Theatre in 2002. Courtesy of Miguel Faleiro.

Why the Gulbenkian Works

According to the Directory of Social Change's 2005 *Guide to the Major Trusts*, the United Kingdom Branch of the Gulbenkian Foundation ranks ninety-second in the UK league table of grant-making charities and foundations. As a whole, the Calouste Gulbenkian Foundation is the third- or fourth-largest in Europe, with assets (according to its 2003 *Annual Report*) of €2,215 million, an annual income of €289 million, and a grants and activities programme of €70 million, but in Britain, where the 300 largest trusts account for £1.1 billion of the £1.9 billion distributed by the trust and foundation community each year, the United Kingdom Branch's £2 million a year grants programme makes it a relatively modest player. Yet, throughout the time we were researching this book, we were regularly told, 'The Gulbenkian punches above its weight.' It is worth concluding by asking why.

There is no doubt that the United Kingdom Branch's unique position as an organisation that behaves like a British charity, but in fact is not one, gives it distinct operational advantages. Having a single Trustee, and one who has executive authority, creates a clear administrative focus. At Portland Place there are none of the 'office politics' associated with a broad-based volunteer board of the Great and the Good. The fact that there were only two London Trustees in the first forty-nine years of its existence, Sir Charles Whishaw and Mikhael Essayan, has created a remarkable continuity, and it is evident that in both cases the Trustees have been willing to back the radical impulses of their staff. On the other hand, the pivotal role of the Trustee as the United Kingdom's sole representative on the Foundation's Board in Lisbon must place a considerable responsibility on that individual. Fortunately the new London Trustee, Martin Essayan, great-grandson of Calouste Sarkis Gulbenkian, seems ready to shoulder the burden.

Although having one Trustee in the United Kingdom means more work for that individual, it allows for clarity of purpose and quick decisions. It also means that from the beginning the Gulbenkian has had to rely on the expertise of professional staff who have worked in the areas of interest to the Foundation. The delegation of decision-taking to London below a certain level of individual grants means that the staff have both responsibility and the security of knowing that they can make the necessary commitments. Having three distinct areas of operation, Arts, Social Welfare, Education –

Portuguese pupils
from Rouge Bouillon
School in Jersey
receiving the Summer
Edition of ACET
Jersey's Portuguese
Newsletter to take
home to their
parents.
Photo: Courtesy of
the *Jersey Evening
Post*

and now with the burgeoning Anglo-Portuguese Cultural Relations Programme, a fourth – the United Kingdom Branch has had to recruit specialists in each of these areas, and while the separate Directorates have never operated in a particularly 'corporate' manner, the Branch has been most successful when the Programmes have run in concert.

Confidence in one's professional role, and sharing a sense of the Gulbenkian's mission with a group of colleagues, has created an appetite for risk, a willingness to support the innovative, and an eye for the neglected. As a secure but not over-large operation, the United Kingdom Branch can fund experimental projects and new ideas in the hope that its investment in research and development will lead to the project being taken up by longer-term funders such as the Arts Council, local authorities or the government. The trick has been to see where one small project has wider application, while the Foundation's publications programme ensures that knowledge is not lost, even when a priority is not taken up elsewhere. As a way of turning theory into practice, the established cycle of a research period, the gathering together of a group of expert advisers, and the communication of policy through the *Annual Report* followed by a five-year-or-so period of grants, with some 'legacy' funding at its conclusion, seems exemplary for an organisation that simply cannot take on the role of a long-term funder. This does not mean that after the first award there will be no other: organisations that establish good relations with the United Kingdom Branch have been able to return with fresh suggestions and found a sympathetic hearing.

The Branch is a remarkably informal organisation, which reflects its tradition of backing people before projects. Entrepreneurial themselves, the staff have sought out the 'social entrepreneurs' who have wanted to create new organisations, influence government policy, change ideas. It has been able to persuade the Great and the Good – Lord Bridges, Dame Eileen Younghusband, Dame Mary Warnock – to chair enquiries and sit on committees, but it has been equally successful in gaining the trust and support of innovators like Michael Young, Helen Crummy from Craigmillar, and John Fox of Welfare State. From the beginning it has been willing to back individual artists, at all stages of their careers, with a confidence that larger organisations have rarely shown. The Foundation's contribution to contemporary art, music, literature, dance and drama in Britain over the past fifty years has been immense, and it has had a knack of backing winners. We have been gratified by the number of times we have discovered that a small grant from the Gulbenkian has led on to greater things.

Above all, the Gulbenkian has had style. Its impressive – and now remarkably inexpensive – offices in Portland Place still have the air of the nineteenth-century American Embassy they once were. Its restaurant no longer exists, and there have been those who were suspicious of its hospitality. But that was what made the Gulbenkian special. It became a place ministers and officials were willing to visit, thus helping the Foundation in its understanding of government, and, as the United Kingdom Branch's financial power shrank in relative terms, it was able to build the alliances with other foundations and agencies that were necessary to sustain the voluntary sector and drive forward the arts. The Foundation remains a hospitable place, and it continues to provide a space in Central London where other organisations can meet. It is through partnership, as well as leadership, that the Gulbenkian has so successfully punched above its weight.

Here we find the Foundation's essential moral purpose: over the past fifty years it has been able to take the broad responsibilities outlined in its founding statutes and to forge Art, Social Welfare, Education and, imaginatively, Science, into a humanitarian partnership at the service of society as a whole. It has been creative and charitable in the best sense of the words. Its monuments are not only buildings, books, paintings, sculptures, drama, music and choreography, they are also institutions, organisations and other charities; but most importantly they are people: people helped, people inspired, people influenced. In achieving this, the United Kingdom Branch of the Gulbenkian Foundation has truly been helping to build a better future.

RNLB *Calouste Gulbenkian*, an improved self-righting lifeboat for Weston-super-Mare, built with Foundation funding in 1959 and launched in the presence of Dr Perdigão. Photo: Royal National Lifeboat Association.

Bibliography of cited works

The principal sources for this book have been personal interviews, the typescript Press Notices issued by the United Kingdom Branch between 1956 and 1970, and the UK Branch's *Annual Reports*, issued in slightly changing formats since 1971. In addition, we have cited a number of specific publications, listed alphabetically by author or editor below. Where a report has become associated with the chairman of a specific enquiry – for instance *Help for the Arts*, 1958 is more generally known as the Bridges Report – we have given the name of the chairman as author/editor of the report. Where a report has no named author, editor, or chair, we have listed it under the originating institution.

Unpublished works

London Branch unpublished internal reports to the Board
Peter Brinson, *Help to Artists*, typescript, October 1979
Richard Mills, internal policy paper 64/7, January 1964
Richard Mills internal policy paper 78/5, January 1966

Personal recollections and memoirs
Lord Annan, letter to Richard Mills, 17 September 1989
Helen Crummy, letter to Richard Mills, 30 June 1992
Lord Feversham, letter to Richard Mills, 5 June 1989
Robin Guthrie, letter to Richard Mills, 19 March 1992
Robert Leaper, letter to Richard Mills, 7 September 1992
Elisabeth Littlejohn, letter to Richard Mills, August 1992
Richard Mills, 'Reminiscences', unpublished typescript, 14 February 1990
Peter Stark, letter to Richard Mills, 9 June 1992
George Wedell, letter to Richard Mills, 31 August 1992
Charles Whishaw, 'A Kind of Lawyer: Some reminiscences', unpublished typescript, 1991

Calouste Gulbenkian Foundation publications

Keith Allen and Phyllida Shaw, *On the Brink of Belonging: A national enquiry into puppetry*, 1992
Sir Colin Anderson (chair), *Training in the Conservation of Paintings*, 1972
Trevor Bailey and Ian Scott, *Rural Arts: A discussion document*, 1989
Andrew Bibby and Saul Becker (eds), *Young Carers in Their Own Words*, 2000
Reg Bolton, *New Circus*, 1987
Alan Bowness, Lawrence Gowing and Phillip James (eds), *54/64: Painting and Sculpture of a Decade*, Calouste Gulbenkian Foundation and Tate Gallery, 1964
Lord Bridges (chair), *Help for the Arts*, 1959
Peter Brinson (chair), *Dance Education and Training in Britain*, 1980
Peter Brinson and Fiona Dick, *Fit to Dance? The report of the national inquiry into dancers' health and injury*, 1996
Rod Brooks, *Wanted! Community Artists*, 1988
John Burnside and Maurice Riordan (eds), *Wild Reckoning: An anthology provoked by Rachel Carson's Silent Spring*, 2004
Calouste Gulbenkian Foundation, *Broadcasting and Youth*, 1979
Calouste Gulbenkian Foundation, *Making a Song and Dance About It: An invitation to use and enjoy the arts in rural areas*, leaflet, 1990
Calouste Gulbenkian Foundation, *Twenty-One Years: An anniversary account of policies and activities 1956–1977 United Kingdom and Commonwealth Branch*, 1977
Peter Coles, *Manchester Hospitals' Arts Project*, 1981

Community Business Ventures Unit, *Whose Business is Business?*, 1981

Graham Devlin, *Beggars' Opera: A discussion document on small-scale touring opera and music-theatre in the UK*, 1992

Rose de Wend Fenton and Lucy Neal, *The Turning World: Stories from the London International Festival of Theatre*, 2005

Christie Dickason, *Experience and Experiment: New theatre workshops 1979–1982*, 1987

Siân Ede (ed.), *Strange and Charmed: Science and the contemporary visual arts*, 2000

Anthony Everitt, *Joining In: An investigation into participatory music*, 1997

Sue Hercombe, *What the hell do we want an artist here for?*, 1986

Bob Hescott, *The Feast of Fools: The story of community theatre in Nottingham*, 1983

Rachel Hodgkin and Peter Newell, *Effective Government Structures for Children*, 1996

Rachel Hodgkin and Peter Newell (eds), *UK Review of Effective Government Structures for Children 2001*, 2001

Philip Hope and Penny Sharland, *Tomorrow's Parents: Developing parenthood education in schools*, 1997

Tess Hurson, *Did We Do That? An evaluation of the Calouste Gulbenkian Foundation's Rural Arts Agency Scheme*, 1996

Sir Gilmour Jenkins (chair), *Making Musicians*, 1965

John A. Kay et al., *Good Cause for Gambling? The prospects for a National Lottery in the UK*, 1992

Owen Kelly, *Digital Creativity*, 1996

Jean La Fontaine, *Bullying: The child's view*, 1991

Jane Lees and Sue Plant, *PASSPORT: A framework for personal and social development*, 2000

Peter Mandelson, *Young People and Broadcasting*, 1981

Jamie McCullough, *Meanwhile Gardens*, 1978

Annette Massie, *Dance in Time*, 1983

Jorge Molder and Rui Sanches, *A Ilha do Tesouro (Treasure Island)*, Centro de Arte Moderna José de Azeredo Perdigão, Fundação Calouste Gulbenkian, Lisbon, 1997

Redmond Mullin, *AIM: A report on the arts initiative and money project 1980–1983*, 1984

Peter Newell, *One Scandal Too Many: The case for comprehensive protection for children in all settings*, 1993

Peter Newell, *Taking Children Seriously: A proposal for a Children's Rights Commissioner*, 1991; fully revised edition, 2000

John Pearce, *At the Heart of the Community Economy: Community enterprise in a changing world*, 1993

John Pearce, *Centres for Curiosity and Imagination: When is a museum not a museum?*, 1998

John Pearce, *Social Enterprise in Anytown*, 2003

Kenneth Rea, *A Better Direction: A national enquiry into the training of directors for theatre, film and television*, 1989

Lord Redcliffe-Maud, *Support for the Arts in England and Wales*, 1976

Rosemary Righter, *Save Our Cities*, 1977

Ken Robinson, *The Arts in Schools: Principles, practice and provision*, 1982; second edition, 1989.

Baroness Seear (chair), *Community Business Works: A report by a working party set up to consider community self-help groups and local productive activity*, 1982

Peter Senior and Jonathan Croall, *Helping to Heal: The arts in health care*, 1993

Jane Steele, Mary Tetlow and Alison Graham, Public Management Foundation, *Public Interest: New models for delivering public services?*, 2003

Sir William Utting (chair), *Children and Violence: Report of the Commission on Children and Violence convened by the Gulbenkian Foundation*, 1995

Lord Vaizey (chair), *Going on the Stage: A report to the Calouste Gulbenkian Foundation on professional training for drama*, 1975

Lord Vaizey (chair), *Training Musicians: A report to the Calouste Gulbenkian Foundation on the training of professional musicians*, 1978

Fiona Williams, ESRC CAVA Research Group, *Rethinking Families*, 2004

Paul Willis, *Moving Culture: An enquiry into the cultural activities of young people*, 1990; full text published by Open University Press as *Common Culture*, 1990

Funded and other publications

Action with Communities in Rural England, *A Rural Arts Handbook: A report for the Calouste Gulbenkian Foundation*, ACRE, 1997

Priscilla Alderson, *Children and Pain*, Action for Sick Children, 1992

Lord Annan (chair), *Report of the Committee on the Future of Broadcasting*, HMSO, 1977

Arts Council of Great Britain, *The Glory of the Garden: The development of the arts in England*, ACGB, 1984

Association of Chief Executives of Voluntary Organisations, *Replacing the State? The case for third sector public service delivery*, ACEVO, 2003

Geraldine M. Aves (chair), *The Voluntary Worker in the Social Services: Report of a committee jointly set up by the National Council of Social Service and the National Institute for Social Work Training*, Allen and Unwin, 1969

Lord Boyle (chair), *Current Issues in Community Work: A study by the Community Work Group*, Routledge and Kegan Paul, 1973

Su Braden, *Artists and People*, Routledge and Kegan Paul, 1978

Peter Brinson (chair), *Arts and Communities: The report of the national inquiry into arts and the community*, Community Development Foundation, 1992

Coin Street Community Builders, *There is another way . . . Coin Street Community Builders: Social enterprise in action*, CSCB, nd

Helen Crummy, *Let The People Sing! A story of Craigmillar*, Helen Crummy, 1992

James Derounian, *Another Country: Real life beyond rose cottage*, National Council for Voluntary Organisations, 1993

Directory of Social Change, A *Guide to the Major Trusts 2005/2006*, DSC, 2005

George Goetschius, *Working with Community Groups: Using community development as a method of social work*, Routledge and Kegan Paul, 1969

Liz Greenhalgh and Ken Worpole, *Park Life: Urban parks and social renewal*, Comedia/Demos, 1995

Richard Gutch, *Contracting in the USA,* National Council for Voluntary Organisations, 1991

Richard Gutch, *Contracting Lessons from the US*, National Council for Voluntary Organisations, 1992

Peter Hall, *Making an Exhibition of Myself*, Sinclair-Stevenson, 1993

Paul Henderson and David Francis (eds), *Rural Action: A collection of community work case studies*, Pluto Press, in association with the Community Development Foundation and ACRE, 1993

HM Treasury, *Every Child Matters*, The Stationery Office, 2003

Owen Kelly, *Community, Art and the State: Storming the citadels*, Comedia, 1984

Naseem Khan, *The Arts Britain Ignores: The arts of ethnic minorities in Britain*, Commission for Racial Equality (originally Community Relations Commission), 1976

Peter Kuenstler, *Community Organisation in Great Britain*, Faber and Faber, 1961

Jennie Lee, *A Policy for the Arts: The first steps*, Cmnd.2601, HMSO, 1965

The Magistrates' Association, *The Welfare of the Child: Assessing evidence in children cases*, MA, 1994

François Matarasso, *Use or Ornament? The social impact of participation in the arts*, Comedia, 1997

Gillian Pugh, Erica De'Ath and Celia Smith, *Confident Parents, Confident Children: Policy and practice in parent education and support*, National Children's Bureau, 1994

Museums, Libraries and Archives Council, *Renaissance in the Regions: A new vision for England's museums*, Resource, 2001

John Myerscough, *The Economic Importance of the Arts in Britain*, Policy Studies Institute, 1988

National Advisory Committee on Creative and Cultural Education, *All Our Futures: Creativity, culture and education*, Department for Education and Skills, 1999

Lord Robbins (chair), *Report of the National Committee of Enquiry into Higher Education*, HMSO, 1963

A.M. Skeffington, *People and Planning*, HMSO, 1969

Caroline Sharp and Lesley Kendall, *Discretionary Awards in Dance and Drama: A survey of local education authorities*, National Foundation for Educational Research, 1996

Francis Spalding, *The Tate: A History*, Tate Publishing, 1998

D.P. Tattum and G. Herbert, *Bullying: A positive response*, Cardiff Institute of Higher Education, 1990; revised edition, 1992

L.C. (Kim) Taylor, *Resources for Learning*, Penguin, 1971

David N. Thomas, *Oil on Troubled Waters: The Gulbenkian Foundation and social welfare*, Directory of Social Change, 1996

David N. Thomas, *The Making of Community Work*, Allen and Unwin, 1983

Peter Townsend, *Meaningful Statistics on Poverty*, Statistical Monitoring Unit, University of Bristol, 1991

Peggy van Praag and Peter Brinson, *The Choreographic Art*, A & C Black, 1963

Ben Whitaker, *The Foundations: An anatomy of philanthropic bodies*, Eyre Methuen, 1974; Pelican 1979.

Ken Worpole, *Towns for People*, Open University Press, 1992 (summary draft report published as *Out of Hours*, Comedia, 1991)

Dame Eileen Younghusband (chair), *Community Work and Social Change: The report of a study group on training set up by the Calouste Gulbenkian Foundation*, Longman, 1968

Calouste Gulbenkian Foundation (UK Branch) publications

AIM: A report on the arts initiative and money project 1980–1983, Redmond Mullin, 1984

Art, not Chance: Nine artists' diaries, Paul Allen (ed.), 2001

Artists in Wigan Schools: A right for all children, Rod Taylor, 1991

The Arts Council Phenomenon: A report of the first-ever Conference of Commonwealth Arts Councils, Jean Battersby, 1981

The Arts in Schools: Principles, practice and provision, Ken Robinson (ed.), 1982; second edition, 1989

The Arts in the Primary School: Reforming teacher education, Malcolm Ross, 1989

At the Heart of the Community Economy: Community enterprise in a changing world, John Pearce, 1993

Beggars' Opera: A discussion document on small-scale touring opera and music-theatre in the UK, Graham Devlin, 1992

A Better Direction: A national enquiry into the training of directors for theatre, film and television, Kenneth Rea, 1989

Black People in Britain: The way forward. A conference report, Rajeev Dhavan (ed.), 1976

Bootstrap: Ten years of enterprise initiatives, Martin McEnery, 1989

The Bottom Line: New prospects for teaching and learning the double bass, Rodney Slatford and Stephen Pettitt, 1985

Broadcasting and Youth: A study commissioned by the British Broadcasting Corporation, the Calouste Gulbenkian Foundation, the Independent Broadcasting Authority and the Manpower Services Commission, 1979

Bullying: The child's view, Jean La Fontaine, 1991

Centres for Curiosity and Imagination: When is a museum not a museum?, John Pearce, 1998

Children and Violence: Report of the Commission on Children and Violence convened by the Gulbenkian Foundation, Sir William Utting (chair), 1995

The Children's Music Book: Performing musicians in school, Saville Kushner, 1991

Community Business Works: A report by a working party set up to consider community self-help groups and local productive activity, Baroness Seear (chair), 1982

Community Challenge: A conference report, 1983

Computers and Arts Management: A paper for discussion, Iwan Williams, 1982

Creating Chances: Arts interventions in Pupil Referral Units and Learning Support Units, Richard Ings, 2004

Crossing the Line: Extending young people's access to cultural venues, John Harland and Kay Kinder (eds), National Foundation for Educational Research, 1999

Dance Education and Training in Britain, Peter Brinson (chair), 1980

Dance in Time: International dance course for professional choreographers and composers 1975–1983, Annette Massie, 1983

Did We Do That? An evaluation of the Calouste Gulbenkian Foundation's Rural Arts Agency Scheme, Tess Hurson, 1996

Digital Creativity, Owen Kelly, 1996

Discretionary Award Provision in England and Wales: A survey carried out by the National Foundation for Educational Research, Felicity Fletcher-Campbell, Wendy Keys and Lesley Kendall, 1994

The Economic Situation of the Visual Artist, 1985

Effective Government Structures for Children: Report of a Gulbenkian Foundation inquiry, Rachel Hodgkin and Peter Newell, 1996

Experience and Experiment: New theatre workshops 1979–1982, Christie Dickason, 1987

A Fairer Hearing: A review of music commissioning in the UK and Ireland, Keith Allen and Phyllida Shaw, 1993

The Feast of Fools: The story of community theatre in Nottingham, Bob Hescott, 1983

54/64: Painting and Sculpture of a Decade, Alan Bowness, Lawrence Gowing and Phillip James (eds), CGF and Tate Gallery, 1964

Fit to Dance? The report of the national inquiry into dancers' health and injury, Peter Brinson and Fiona Dick, 1996

Funding Options and Opportunities in the Republic of Ireland: A report prepared for the Calouste Gulbenkian Foundation, Stephen Rourke, 1989

Going on the Stage: A report to the Calouste Gulbenkian Foundation on professional training for drama, Lord Vaizey (chair), 1975

Good Cause for Gambling? The prospects for a National Lottery in the UK, John A. Kay et al., 1992

Havens and Springboards: The Foyer movement in context, Colin Ward, 1997

Help for the Arts: A report to the Calouste Gulbenkian Foundation, Lord Bridges (chair), 1959

Helping to Heal: The arts in health care, Peter Senior and Jonathan Croall, 1993

Here Today, Here Tomorrow: Helping schools to promote attendance, Susan Hallam and Caroline Roaf, 1995

Home – A Place for Work?, Richmond Postgate, 1984

Hospice without Walls: The story of West Cumbria's remarkable Hospice at Home service, Andrew Bibby, 1999

Investing in Local Enterprise Development: A new perspective for the UK, CGF in conjunction with CEI Consultants Ltd, 1989

Joining In: An investigation into participatory music, Anthony Everitt, 1997

Latent Talent: In search of talent in the arts outside the formal education sector, Phyllida Shaw, 1999

Lets Act Locally: The growth of Local Exchange Trading Systems, Jonathan Croall, 1997

Local Enterprise and the Unemployed, Robert Davies and Rupert Nabarro, 1986

Locked in – Locked out: The experience of young offenders out of society and in prison, Angela Neustatter, 2002

Making Musicians: A report to the Calouste Gulbenkian Foundation, Sir Gilmour Jenkins (chair), 1965

Manchester Hospitals' Arts Project, Peter Coles, 1981

Meanwhile Gardens, Jamie McCullough, 1978

Mediation in Action: Resolving court disputes without trial, Hazel Genn, 1999

Moving Culture: An enquiry into the cultural activities of young people, Paul Willis, 1990; full text published by Open University Press as *Common Culture*, 1990

Music in Between: An investigation into the opportunities for training, rehearsal, performance and promotion available to creative performing musicians, Tony Haynes with David Laing and Julie Eaglen, 1989

A National Centre for Community Development: The report of a working party to the Calouste Gulbenkian Foundation, Hywel Griffiths (chair), 1984

The Needs of Youth in Stevenage: A report to the Calouste Gulbenkian Foundation, E.T. Williams (chair), 1959

New Circus, Reg Bolton, 1987

New Town, Home Town: The lessons of experience, Colin Ward, 1993

Nobody Nicked 'Em: How we started a toy library in the East End of London, Joanna Grana, 1983

'. . . Not a Bed of Roses': An arts development officer in the Trade Union Movement, Clare Higney, 1985

On the Brink of Belonging: A national enquiry into puppetry, Keith Allen and Phyllida Shaw, 1992

One Scandal Too Many: The case for comprehensive protection for children in all settings, Peter Newell, 1993

Only Connect: The arts provision system in the UK, Keith Diggle, 1980

The Oxford Internship Scheme: Integration and partnership in initial teacher education, Peter Benton (ed.), 1990

Parents in Secondary Education: The parent organiser project at Westminster City School, Berry Mayall, 1990

PASSPORT: A framework for personal and social development, Jane Lees and Sue Plant, 2000

Patron or Paymaster? The Arts Council dilemma, Elizabeth Sweeting, 1983

Peace at the Last: A survey of terminal care in the United Kingdom. A report to the Calouste Gulbenkian Foundation, H.L. Glyn Hughes, 1960

Preserve or Destroy: Tourism and the environment, Jonathan Croall, 1995

Provision for the Arts in the Republic of Ireland: Report of an inquiry carried out during 1974–5 throughout the twenty-six counties of the Republic of Ireland, Sir James Richards, CGF and An Chomhairle Ealaíon, 1976

Public Interest: New models for delivering public services?, Jane Steele, Mary Tetlow and Alison Graham, Public Management Foundation, 2003

Resource Centres for Community Groups, Marilyn Taylor, CGF and Community Projects Foundation, 1983

Rethinking Families, Fiona Williams, ERSC CAVA Research Group, 2004

Rural Arts: A discussion document, Trevor Bailey and Ian Scott, 1989

Save Our Cities, Rosemary Righter, 1977

Science, not Art: Ten scientists' diaries, Jon Turney (ed.), 2003

Serious Play: An evaluation of arts activities in Pupil
Referral Units and Learning Support Units, Anne Wilkin,
Caroline Gulliver and Kay Kinder, National Foundation
for Educational Research, 2005

Social Enterprise in Anytown, John Pearce, 2003

Special Theatre: The work of Interplay Community Theatre
for people with severe learning difficulties 1970–1985,
Dick Downing and Tony Jones, 1989

Strange and Charmed: Science and the contemporary
visual arts, Siân Ede (ed.), 2000

Support for the Arts in England and Wales: A report to the
Calouste Gulbenkian Foundation, Lord Redcliffe-Maud,
1976

Taking Children Seriously: A proposal for a Children's
Rights Commissioner, Peter Newell, 1991; fully revised
edition, 2000

Teachers for the Inner City, John Raynor, 1981

Teleworking: Thirteen journeys to the future of work,
Andrew Bibby, 1995

Tomorrow's Parents: Developing parenthood education in
schools, Philip Hope and Penny Sharland, 1997

Training in the Conservation of Paintings: Report of a
committee to consider the establishment of an
Institute for training in the conservation of paintings
and drawings, Sir Colin Anderson (chair), 1972

Training Musicians: A report to the Calouste Gulbenkian
Foundation on the training of professional musicians,
Lord Vaizey (chair), 1978

The Turning World: Stories from the London International
Festival of Theatre, Rose de Wend Fenton and Lucy
Neal, 2005

Twenty-One Years: An anniversary account of policies and
activities 1956–1977 United Kingdom and
Commonwealth Branch Calouste Gulbenkian
Foundation, 1977

UK Review of Effective Government Structures for
Children 2001: A Gulbenkian Foundation report,
Rachel Hodgkin and Peter Newell (eds), 2001

Vandalism and Graffiti: The state of the art,
Frank Coffield, 1991

Voluntary Organisations Facing Change: The report of a
project to help Councils for Voluntary Service respond
to local government reorganisation, John Lansley,
1976

Wanted! Community Artists: A summary of principles and
practice for running training schemes for community
artists, with special reference to the Apprenticeship
Scheme (1984–8) set up by the Calouste Gulbenkian
Foundation, Rod Brooks, 1988

What the hell do we want an artist here for?,
Sue Hercombe, 1986

Whose Business is Business? A report by the Community
Business Venture Unit commissioned by the Calouste
Gulbenkian Foundation and the Manpower Services
Commission, 1981

Why Restorative Justice? Repairing the harm caused by
crime, Roger Graef, 2001

Wild Reckoning: An anthology provoked by Rachel
Carson's Silent Spring, John Burnside and Maurice
Riordan (eds), 2004

Wise Before the Event: Coping with crises in schools,
William Yule and Anne Gold, 1993

The Work of Art: A summary of The Economic Importance
of the Arts in Britain, a research study in four volumes
by John Myerscough, Peter Rodgers, CGF and Policy
Studies Institute, 1989

Young Carers in Their Own Words, Andrew Bibby and
Saul Becker (eds), 2000

Young People and Broadcasting: Commissioned from the
British Youth Council by the Calouste Gulbenkian
Foundation, Peter Mandelson, 1981

Index

Page numbers in *italics* refer to illustrations

The authors

Robert Hewison has written widely on nineteenth- and twentieth-century British cultural history. He was Slade Professor of Fine Art at Oxford University, taught English Literature at Lancaster University, and is a regular contributor to *The Sunday Times*. He is an Associate of the independent think-tank Demos. His books include: *Culture and Consensus: England art and politics since 1940* (Methuen, 1997), *Towards 2010* (Arts Council England, 2000), *Ruskin's Venice* (Pilkington Press, 2000), and, with John Holden, *The Right to Art* (Demos, 2004) and *Challenge and Change* (Demos 2005).

John Holden is Head of Culture at the think-tank Demos, a member of the Management Committee of the Clore Leadership Programme, and a Fellow of the RSA. He has been involved in numerous major cultural research projects and recent publications include: *Creative Reading* and *Capturing Cultural Value* (both Demos, 2004), and *Cultural Value and the Crisis of Legitimacy* (Demos, 2006).